AF252067

HEALING THRU ART

My Journey to Self-Love

Art Therapy and DBT therapy working together to heal me from a debilitating eating disorder and trauma.

By Kathleen Kaufman, MA-ATR

PUBLISHED BY NICO 11 PUBLISHING & DESIGN
MUKWONAGO, WISCONSIN
www.nico11publishing.com

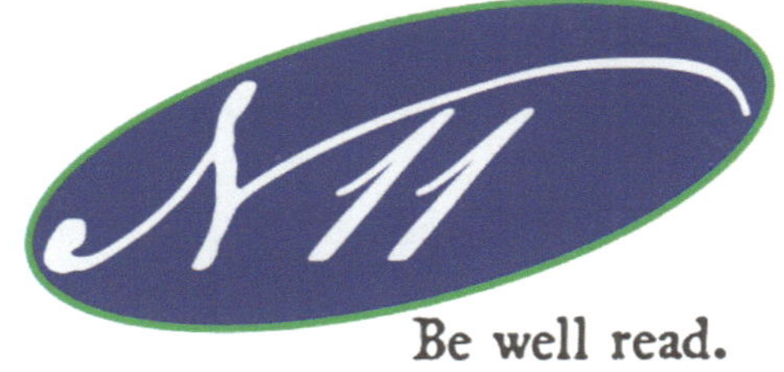

Healing Thru Art

My Journey to Self-Love

Author: Kathleen Kaufman, MA-ATR
Contributing Authors: Dr. Laura Lees, Neal Moglowsky
Contributing Editor: Michael Nicloy
Foreword: Dr. Laura Lees
Associate Editor: Jennifer Guerrero
Proofreader: Lyda Rose Haerle
Cover Design and Interior Layout: Michael Nicloy
Marketing Coordinator: Brenda Brito
marketinginfo@healingthruart.net

ISBN-13: 978-1-945907-77-7

Published by Nico 11 Publishing & Design
Mukwonago, Wisconsin
www.nico11publishing.com

Quantity and wholesale order requests can be emailed to:
mike@nico11publishing.com
or be made by phone: 217.779.9677

Printed in The United States of America

To my husband, Ken, who never wavered in his patience. He stood beside me through the most challenging of times.

My eyes are wide open, and I can see that my pain and suffering were his as well.

I cannot give enough thanks for the support and love he provided for me.

My boys, Cody and Zachary: if it wasn't for them, I would not be here to share this journey.

Every day they brought joy to my heart. Their love gave me more strength than any words could say.

I may have not been perfect, but I did the best I could, and when I look at my children, I know that I got something in my life perfectly right.

There was so much love surrounding me with my husband and my boys, it's an unconditional love… only a mother can understand. My heart is so full with the love I have for my boys, just saying it brings tears to my eyes. They kept me strong as I found the path needed to experience the journey to self-love.

I learned my husband showed me true love, and the boys showed me what pure love meant.

To me the best thing to hold onto in life is my husband, and boys, and my family.

Acknowledgments

Family is extremely important to me. This is why I am starting by thanking my parents. My father, Francis (Joe), and my mother, Laura Belle, have meant the world to me. They have taught me to wake up each morning with a purpose, to never give up, and to be there for my family, for they will always be there for me. I also want to acknowledge my siblings, Millie, Mike, Dale, Terry, Scott, and Mark. I found that each of my siblings provided me new ways to see things; these were special gifts that I took on my journey to health. Everyone brings something different to the table.

My family consists of my siblings and their spouses and ex-spouses; and my nieces and nephews, and their spouses. They are all very important to me. I feel this was the true legacy of my parents who believed very much in family. I saw a quote that fit my family and my parents' beliefs. It was written by Daniel Long, and it says, "So much of what is best in us is bound up in our love of family, that it remains the measure of our stability because it measures our sense of loyalty."

I also have a special place in my heart for my daughter-in-law. The first time I met her, she showed me that it's okay to stand up and speak what you believe in, and still have love and respect for others as you listen to their views; and more importantly, she showed me the love and support she has for my son—with the connection of God, they stand strong together.

I can't forget my friends that are like the extra sisters who I chose myself: Amber, Brenda, Jennifer, Deb, Lauren, Laurie, Kathleen, Kelliy, DeDe, and Sandy. Some, like Sandy and Laurie, have known me for over 30 years. Their friendship is like gold; they are the type of friends who stick with you through thick and thin. They have been with me through much of the struggle I endured; I'm sure with questions, worry, and confusion. Yet, even today when we meet, they are the friends who carry on as if there are no worries. They bring laughter to my life, which brings tears of joy to my eyes. I found their love and friendship never stopped; they provided their support, and never judged, but were always there beside me. The others are also extremely close friends, whose friendships helped me walk through my journey. These friends are priceless as they have been by my side with strength, hope, and encouragement. The biggest support I found from them all was they brought me the joys of life, including times of tears and times of laughter. These women and their friendship are a gift of a lifetime.

My publisher and editor, Michael Nicloy, owner of Nico 11 Publishing & Design, is helping me reach one of my major goals in life and healing. My goal in life has always been to help others. This path of mine may have taken some unexpected turns, but it never changed my goal. Mike sat and listened as I shared my experiences. He learned about the effects that both a severe eating disorder and trauma have on a person.

Mike's enthusiasm and leadership have helped guide me through the writing of this book. I was eager to share this book as Mike walked me through the steps of putting the details together. He leads with compassion, which brings more to the process than someone just pushing a pencil. It was like I met up with an ol' friend talking about my highs and lows of life. Mike listened, as if he were living the experience all over again with me, and he was just as eager to bring his expertise to the process. I thank Mike for helping me meet my dreams and goal to help others.

I thank my whole Treatment Team. There are so many individuals who fall under this role, but a special thanks to Dr. R. Watson; Dr. Heaton; Dr. Joan Russo; my dietitian, Melanie; and Rich, my Trainer from the YMCA. And I also want to give a sincere thank you to every person who has helped me along the way.

A Very Special Thanks to Neal and Dr. Laura:

I would not have ever made it this far, or have been able to put the words together in this book, without the help from two extraordinary professionals who not only educated me, but listened, nurtured, and inspired me. They helped me find a life that I am proud of and that is truly worth living:

Neal Moglowsky has a Master's Degree in Educational Psychology and is a Licensed Professional Counselor (LPC). He is intensively trained in Dialectical Behavior Therapy (DBT) and is a Linehan-Certified DBT Clinician. He is president of the Center for Behavioral Medicine; and he is my therapist. Neal steadily guided me and, at times, took my hand as he led me to the work I needed to learn and experience. We worked hard together to break down my barriers and myths that prevented me from growing. Neal not only validated my experience, he also demonstrated what I cherished and believed in people. My belief since childhood was that most people are dedicated and good-hearted, and care about others. Neal helped me to find this belief again, to trust and believe in good. He was also someone I learned to trust, and whom I could share the scariest and darkest moments in my life's experience. In return, he brought me insight to self-compassion and trust in myself.

My journey, with the guidance and knowledge of Neal standing there beside me, was invaluable. I thank Neal. He will have a special place in my heart for the rest of my life. I will even treasure the bumps in the road that we often encountered when he would say that I "missed the mark." I was determined to meet his determination with hard work as I found balance and meaning to my experiences. I will also remember the look on his face when he would be frustrated with me, AND state that his head was about to blow up. It was Neal who showed me that I had love for myself all along...it just needed to be uncovered.

Dr. Laura Lees, PysD, is a clinical psychologist, and is one of the top Certified Eating Disorder Specialists in Milwaukee, Wisconsin. Laura challenged my eating disorder thoughts as we worked on healthy life goals. She took away my scale, which helped me to unlock the chains that kept me stuck in my eating disorder. She also took scale two, and three, and all the others I bought and handed in to her. From being ruled by numbers to freedom, Laura educated me on the importance of nutritional balance for both emotional and physical wellbeing. Laura inspired me, she often was straight forward, and she kept me on track (which was difficult at times, since I changed topics often). I realize now what a master I was in changing the direction of our discussions when things were difficult or evoked too many feelings. Laura was never fooled; she always brought me back to work on any challenging topic. Laura is a strong woman in what she believes; she has a lot of charisma. Her professionalism and passion make her a delight to work with. She is in a class of her own.

These two incredible individuals helped me put the pieces of my life's puzzle together in a way that I could understand, and incorporate them into my life's journey. My deepest appreciation to you both.

Table of Contents

Foreword

Dr. Laura A. Lees

Clinical Psychologist
Certified Eating Disorder Specialist

I remember two questions that kept coming to mind after completing Kathleen's initial assessment: How does someone with 40-plus years of a chronic eating disorder know literally nothing about food? And, after the trauma she endured, how is this woman even still alive? You'll understand why I wondered this as her journey unfolds.

Kathleen was referred to me by Neal Maglowsky, LPC, a psychotherapist and certified Dialectical Behavior Therapist. While it is unusual for a non-DBT clinician like me to serve as a co-therapist in the Linehan DBT model, Neal and I had success working together with several other patients who had chronic eating disorders for whom traditional outpatient psychotherapy and hospital treatment programs did not work.

When I first met Kathleen, I was 25 years into a career as a specialist dedicated to helping people recover from eating disorders and other associated mental health issues. She had already had numerous mental health hospitalizations and several medical hospitalizations, including one for a month-long coma. I was surprised by my initial thought: *How am I going to help Kathleen?*

As you begin to read this book, you will find it hard to put down. As Kathleen challenged her eating disorder, her excruciating trauma, and her health complications, her desire was to not only change, but *really* change—even when it meant facing insurmountable fears that she had convinced herself she would never, ever unveil. This book is a must-read for anyone treating patients with, or personally experiencing any form of trauma, eating disorder, addiction, or other mental health issue. It not only benefits those with similar struggles, but it's a wonderful resource for doctors, psychologists, general therapists, and Art Therapists who are working with clients faced with similar life experiences.

What you will learn from this book will include how a devastating eating disorder affects a person. You will also be introduced to Dialectical Behavior Therapy (DBT), and how Kathleen broke down her new acquired DBT skills into steps of creating art and processing her work along with her therapists.

Kathleen is a registered Art Therapist (ATR), with a master's degree in administration/education, a Principal's License, and she was an international speaker in the field of education. She was passionate about making a difference with her special needs clients until her life, career, and health crumbled.

Kathleen realized she had the ability to change. This awareness was invigorating and became a highly motivating force for her, because she was finally making progress in therapy. She worked incredibly hard with Neal and me to move from living in absolute fear of food and memories of trauma every single day, to becoming the "strong, loving, and courageous woman" she saw she had the potential to be.

Nutrition was healing her body and brain. Her nutritional deficiency left her unable to see in color and she could only complete her art in black and white. She was finally able to appreciate how much emotion her art was expressing when, for so many years, she could not see it, especially when she fell into that "black and white" stage of drawing. With nutrition in place, she stated it was like a light switch turning on, and she's could see color again.

When she started showing me the art that is found on the following pages, we processed the thoughts and feelings behind those pieces. Together we were able to explore the connections between the eating disorder and trauma in ways that gave her a deeper understanding of how those life experiences affected the ways she felt and functioned in the world.

Kathleen's is an undeniable story of hope for anyone who suffers from an eating disorder and trauma, especially one that has been enduring. It is a testimonial to the grit and tenacity that can be unleashed in a patient when there is a willingness by therapists to step outside of traditional silos of expertise and collaborate in unique ways. It is a testimonial to bringing the patient's passion into therapy and using it to understand lived experience as well as to promote change. Whether you are in therapy or not, or if you are a therapist, never underestimate the capacity for change, even in the estimated 25% assumed to never recover.

Kathleen continues to work on body image and self-acceptance, which sometimes pulls her into patterns of restricting, but she also gets herself back to balanced eating. Although I was initially skeptical about what would change after 40 years, the progress Kathleen has made in both her eating disorder and her trauma recovery is entirely because, deep down, she has always been an amazing reservoir of resiliency, stubborn determination; and she refused to quit on life.

Kathleen's excitement to share her story, her therapy, and her art in an effort to help others is who she is at her core: determined to find any and every avenue to make life easier for others, especially those who know the pain of trauma and eating disorders like she does. I now know there are many reasons why Kathleen survived when all the odds were against her. This inspirational story of personal transformation is just one of them!

Dr. Lees received her Doctor of Psychology degree with honors, is a Certified Eating Disorders Specialist, and was named one of the top leading experts in eating disorders in Milwaukee Magazine's *"A Guide to Top Psychotherapists."*

Introduction

Within this book you will learn about my journey, which has been a lifetime of struggle with an eating disorder, exacerbated by trauma. What seemed to be a successful life became a downward spiral filled with pain and suffering.

I write about my use of Art Therapy as a tool to express myself when no words could. Art Therapy became my tool with which I could express my personal feelings and thoughts. In addition to Art Therapy, I will discuss the benefits from the new skills I acquired during therapy, the skills that are the basis of Dialectical Behavior Therapy (DBT), created by American psychologist Marsha Linehan. This type of psychotherapy combines both behavioral science and Buddhist concepts, including skills such as mindfulness and self-acceptance, both of which were huge factors in my journey from hell to self-compassion. The Art Therapy and the DBT skills discussed in this book have created a new understanding and a new connection which brought meaning to my own life experience. This book was designed to share how my art process and some new skills that I have been acquiring have helped me work through the stumbling blocks of life, while still accepting that life itself is full of obstacles. I believe that I am now reaching for a new goal, which is to share my story in this book to help others who, like me, desperately want to get out of suffering. The connections from my debilitating eating disorder and trauma, to my journey with Art and DBT Therapies, gave me the determination and strength needed to survive. It is my desire that this book will help provide the stepping-stones that others may need to make the journey from self-hate to self-love.

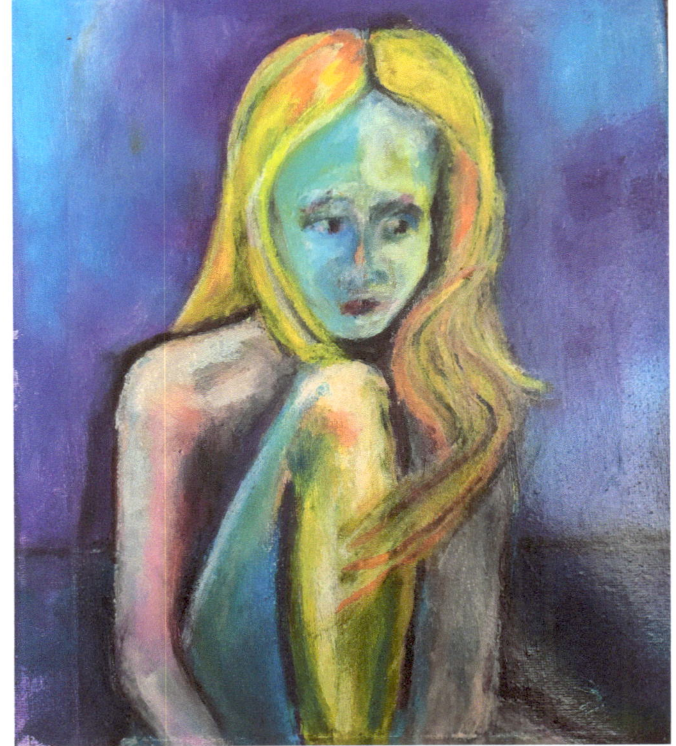

The Struggle

I chose the following paintings for the front and the back covers. To me, they represent who I was to who I have become on this journey to self-love.

Strong, Loving, Courageous Woman

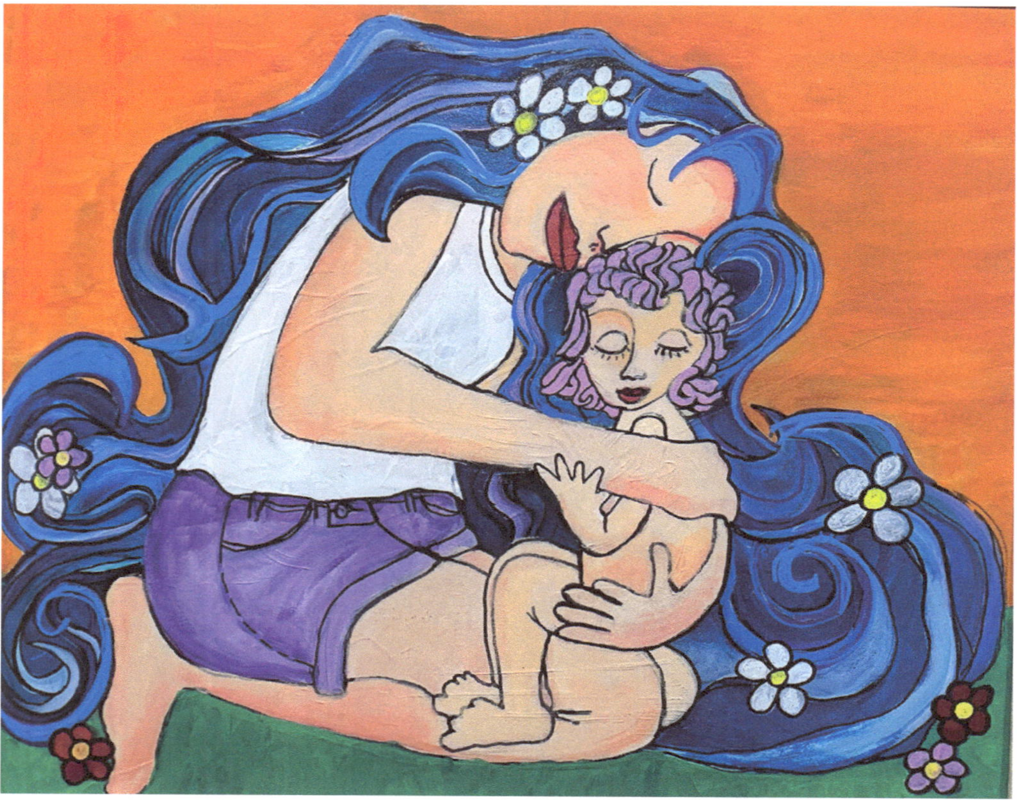

The first painting on the cover, *Strong, Loving, Courageous Woman*, represents my growth as I found strength to nurture my inner child and to be loving to myself. I learned to trust and accept the love I had for myself and from others. The painting was to emulate the journey of healing. When asked by my therapist, "What do you want to be?" I said, "I want to be a strong, loving, and courageous woman." This painting shows me as a woman embracing my inner child, who is so desperately seeking validation and love. The painting marks the point of my journey that demonstrates my determination to accept myself and my identity. Art Therapy gave me a voice to express gratitude and my emotions, and assisted me with an avenue to understanding the skills my therapist was providing me. It also helped me to articulate and challenge my thoughts and beliefs that were instilled in me as I grew older and began my ongoing struggle with my eating disorder, which was later exacerbated by trauma. This painting is my expression of my joy as I fought for a life worth living. This strong, loving, courageous woman validates who I am—inside and out.

The Naked Woman Blues depicts how I had to fight for my identity. I was so stuck in shame that I was not able to find who I was. I never wanted people to see this side of me.

As someone who has suffered the trauma of abuse and a debilitating eating disorder, I found myself researching online to see if there were other women who also suffered from eating disorders and/or trauma. I found I was not alone. There are many individuals who have had similar experiences. They have also struggled with a sense of humiliation and shame. I painted this naked woman to express those emotions. I still find at times I get triggered when I see my own reflection. This reaction tells me I still have work to do on my poor self-image. I discovered that utilizing the process of Art Therapy has helped me to express what was inexpressible in any other format. It helped me to reveal my inner secrets and build a stronger connection with those I love.

When I painted this figure, I was trying to show a woman who struggled with shame and the lack of self-acceptance. The painting is of a woman with her

The Naked Woman Blues

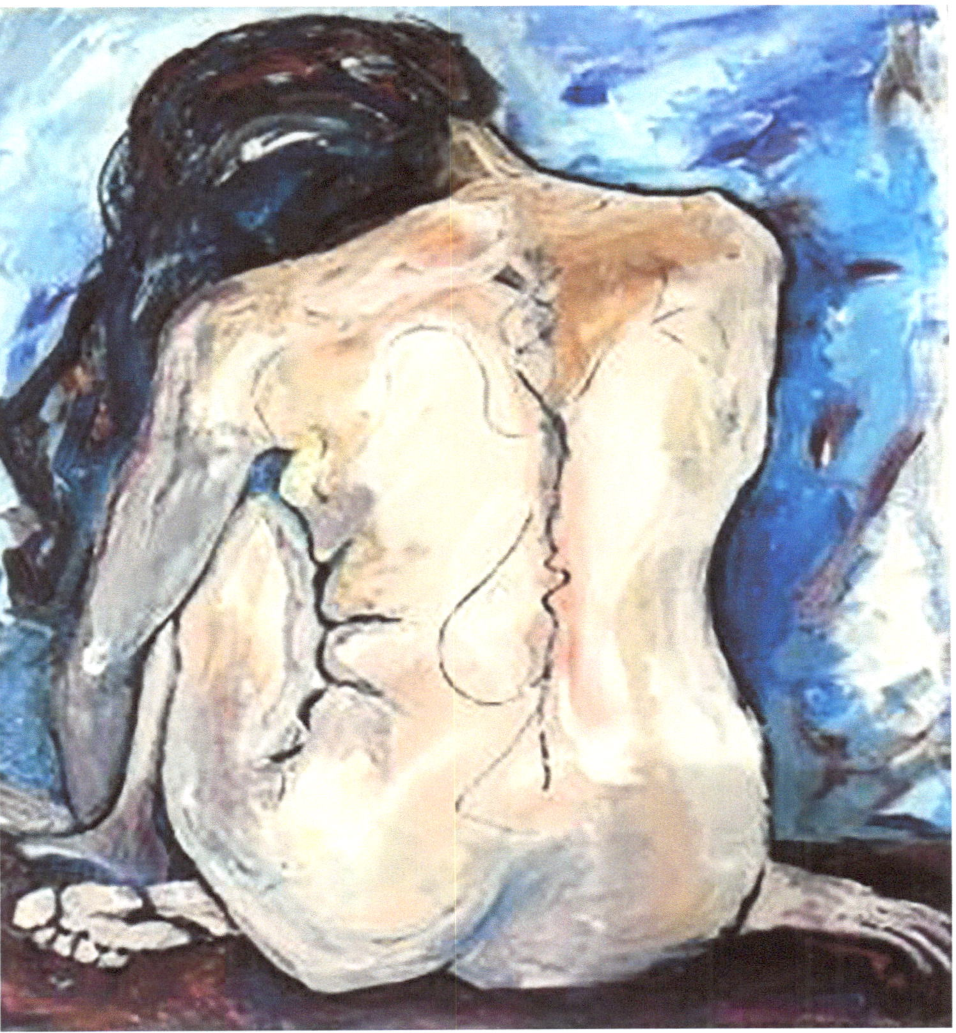

legs curled up as she holds herself tight, hiding from her fear of life and shame. This depicts how I was and how I lived my life, which was so full of fear. My fear and shame festered until it turned into self-hate and fear. There was no room for self-acceptance. My negativity and fear even blocked positive comments from others. I couldn't believe the words anyone said to me. I naturally twisted their comments, so their words would fit my beliefs, even if they were distorted or full of shame.

I got myself so wrapped up in the feeling of shame, I became trapped in a world of self-hate, which I turned inwardly, and I was screaming for help. When this happened, I built enough negative beliefs, thoughts, and memories that it was like a broken record playing in my head over and over. This recording continued to play all of my negative thoughts and kept me trapped in suffering. This period of my life was ruled by shame, self-loathing, and self-hate.

Society Hype (*back cover painting*)

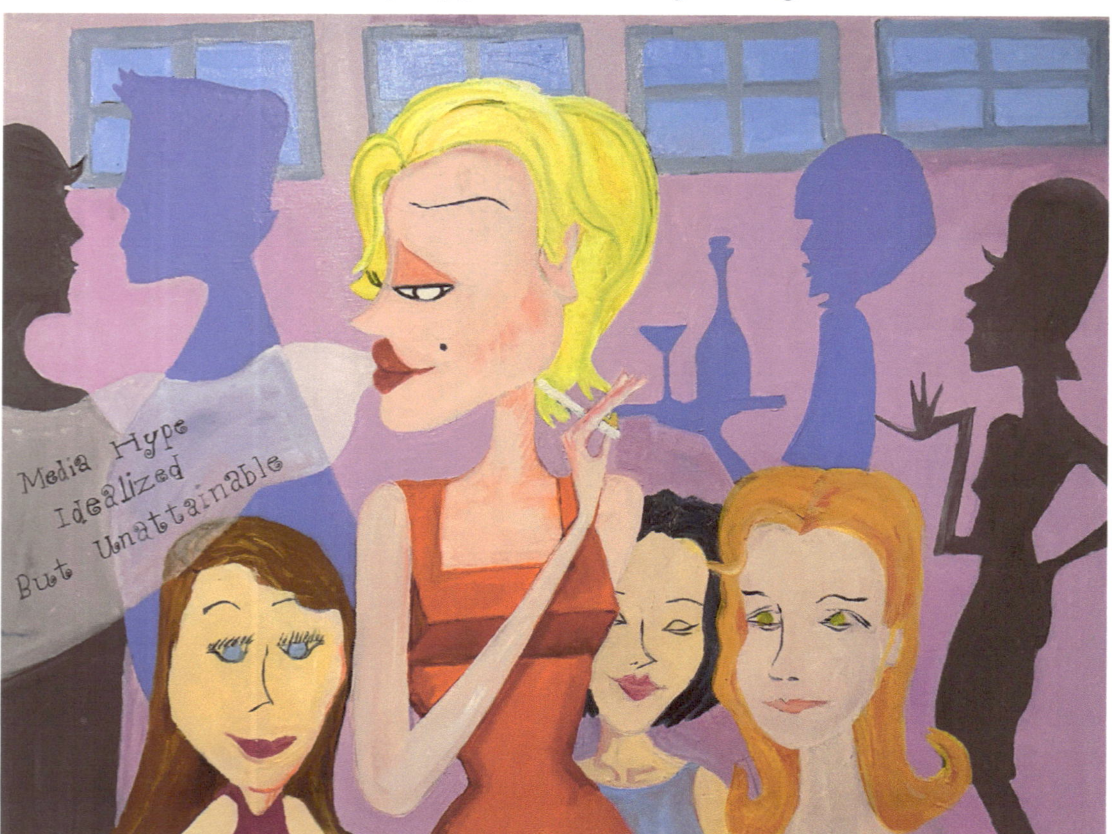

Society Hype was painted to represent what I believed about what society expected successful women to act and look like. I truly believed the propaganda, but the truth lies in the smoked-filled view, "Society hype was idolized but unattainable." Over the years, society had created distorted pictures in magazines with photoshopped images of women so thin and contrived, which was simply not reality. It was obvious in magazines that images were touched up and elongated. Society was causing every young girl and woman to believe that if they looked like this, then they too would be strong, successful, and beautiful—and possibly causing them to die trying to reach this myth. I didn't know it at the time, but it was my anger at society that manifested this painting. I didn't realize that part of my eating disorder was also pulled into this belief, and I strived for this so-called success and beauty. I strived for success and didn't realize I was becoming just the opposite, as my eating disorder created a sick and frail individual. I was so vulnerable that I became prey, too meek to ward off a determined predator. I was sucked into society's distortion, and it pulled me deeper into my illness. I didn't realize how narrow my focus had become and how the illness kept me numb from the world as I tried to live up to society's terms of success.

When I look at this painting now, it creates in me so much anger about how society captured the hopes and dreams of young girls and women who wanted to be successful, yet in reality this distortion was unattainable. I would like to be a pioneer of sorts, to help the world's view to continue on a path to a healthier stance for women. Let women be successful no matter what they look like, or what their size may be—what is within them is what makes them successful.

CHAPTER ONE

My Story Starts

As a young woman, I was full of life—a daughter, a sister, a wife, and a mother. I was determined to be strong and successful. I was a Registered Art Therapist and a supervisor in the world of education. Knowing that I was a young woman in a very male-dominated field, I realized that, to be heard, I needed to further my education, especially if I was going to be able to make a difference. I went back to school and earned my master's in administration/education, with my Principal License. Strong and determined, I had a skip in my walk—I felt I could tackle almost anything.

I was eager to provide opportunities and avenues to succeed for individuals with special needs. I enjoyed creating large activities which allowed individuals to see their abilities, not their disabilities. I had a philosophy of "never say no, there's a way." I have my younger brother to thank for that. My brother was born deaf, and I can remember his standing alongside my mother as they fought for his rights to learn side-by-side with his peers and to be included in many of the school's activities. He participated in track and the bowling league; and he competed on the local YMCA's diving team. He made me want to stand tall and help provide other individuals with the same hopes and dreams he had, and the opportunities needed to succeed. This is where "never say no, there's a way" came to life. My brother and my mother fighting for his rights fueled me, as a young child, with the determination I needed to find new avenues and ways to adapt to any situation, along with teaching others to provide these opportunities for growth.

It was already so clear, at a young age, that I wanted to help as many individuals with disabilities as best I could. This was a time in my life when I was full of energy and I *had* to succeed. I wanted to make a difference for individuals. I carried this attitude of *I have to* throughout my life. It was a life pattern which was leading me down a path of Go-Go-Go.

I kept this pattern of needing to be on the go constantly, even while secretly keeping an eating disorder hidden from the world. I thought it was what kept me going and led me to much success in life. For a very long time I never realized I had an eating disorder. It wasn't even denial. It was just a way of life.

As I aged, I hit a few bumps in the road and was faced with the possibility that I might have an eating disorder. I viewed this so-called "eating disorder" as a *functional* eating disorder (if there is such a thing). Even then, I believed I was in what I called the height of my career.

Negative thoughts of self were already present in me as an adolescent. I was also struggling, at this very young age, with the early signs of an eating disorder, which I hadn't realized then. When I was older, I found out my parents just thought I ate funny, which did sometimes bring frustration and anger at the dinner table. As an adolescent, I was struggling with the unknown, and all alone with my secret behaviors. Having an eating disorder was unknown territory for anyone—even doctors. As time went on, the term "eating disorder" came up, and my parents told me that the dentist actually was the first to identify my struggles. Because even though I was just an adolescent, my eating disorder was already taking a toll on my teeth.

I created the following two prints when I was in high school. They are just so strong. Even back then I captured my lack of self-identity; I wasn't in touch with these feelings or emotions at the time. I was showing my deep thoughts of negativity and self-loathing, and the long search of not knowing who I was as a person. I had to keep my behaviors and thoughts secret. I would say most people who knew me as an adolescent saw a vibrant, high-energy, young lady. What most people didn't see was my self-loathing, negative self-image or the mask that I was wearing on the outside, to hide what was frustrating on the inside.

No Identity

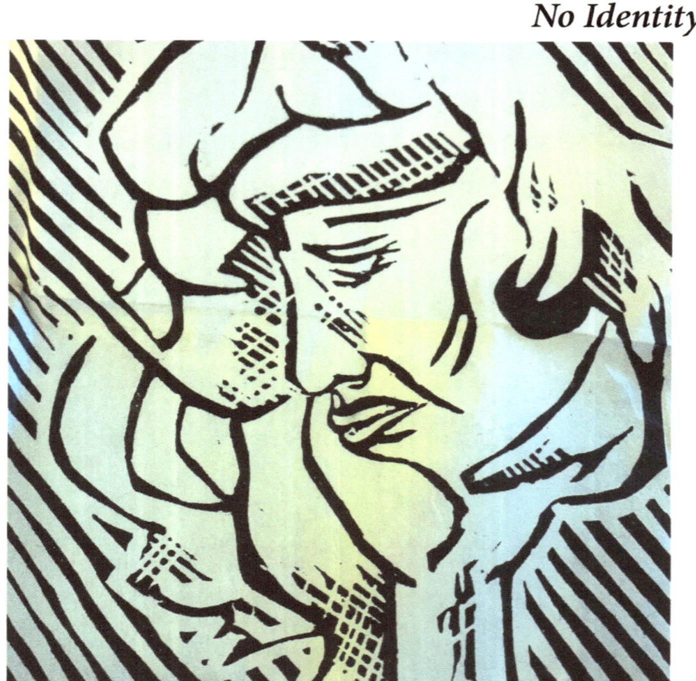

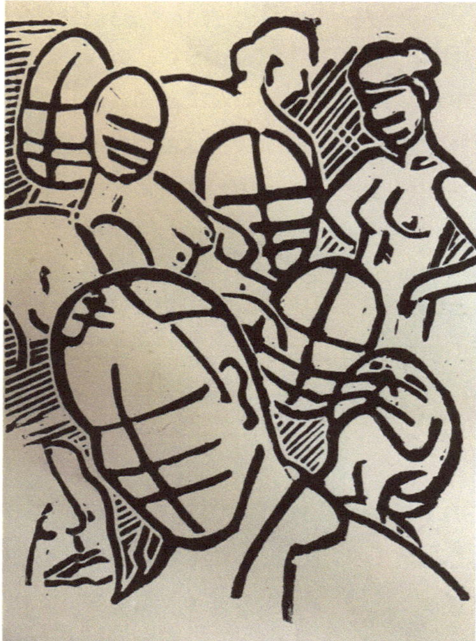

I felt I could conquer anything, until one night, when my world was turned upside down. The assault on my body as a young, naïve woman, overpowered by the perpetrator, was too much for me to handle. To survive, I used what I now know is called dissociating, and that probably saved my life. But at the same time, I turned everything over to my eating disorder. I lived the life of fear and constant suffering,

A crime was committed against me. I kept the trauma I endured from that crime a secret, and it remained a secret from everyone for a very long time. Even now, with so many years passed, I have kept the secret with me; I have only shared a little of it with a few people, and I am still not able to legally talk about it, since the case was settled out of court and a gag order was put in place.

I felt trust was a blurred line. This life-changing experience caused me physical, emotional, spiritual, and psychological harm. It was so distressing it turned my life upside down. I was constantly feeling threatened, and full of fear daily. It was time to work on healing.

Faced with Trauma

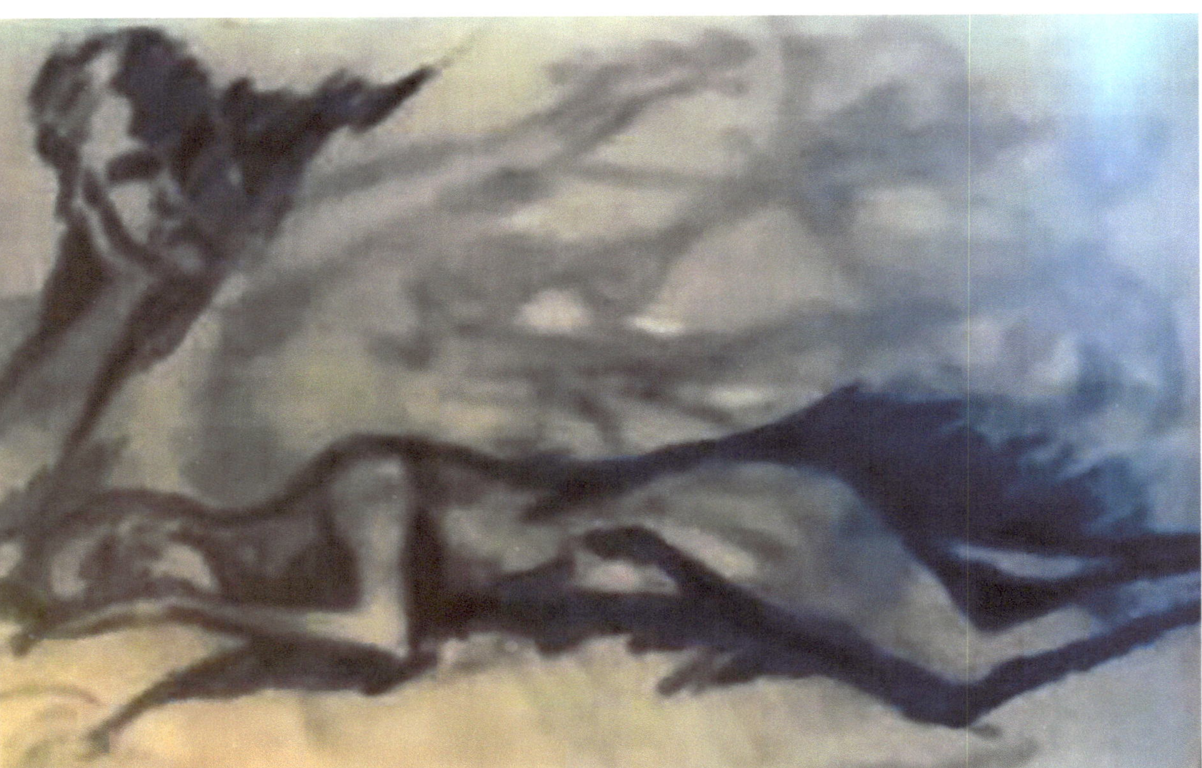

I found this pencil sketch recently in one of my journals, it was completed back when my case was settled. I never realized the importance of my paintings, drawings, or even my doddles. I never knew the paintings I did kept the words I could not speak; they held so much more meaning to me so many years later. I worked with my first therapist during all this. She was like a mother figure to me; I respected her so much. When I look back to when I worked with her, I knew she was always there for me. She was just what I needed at that time. I was living a life of fear and anxiety, and she comforted me. She was extremely dedicated. My husband remembers when I was in a coma for thirty days, she came and spent most of one day trying to help sooth my anxiety to help me come out of the coma. She taped herself talking to me so later the nurses could continue to replay it. The nurses talked about that with me, and how they never saw such dedication. I was proud to work with her, she was just what I needed at that time in my life, as I stood there lost and scared.

More recently I started to begin working with Neal as my therapist. He brought a lot of insight, and education of the skills I needed to start my journey as I worked toward a much healthier me. Neal then asked Dr. Laura Lees, who specializes in eating disorders, to collaborate with him on my therapy. Both Neal and Dr. Laura could see what was blind to me. Dr. Laura explained how important it was to rescue my brain by refeeding it. With refeeding my brain, I was able to work more closely with Neal and his therapeutic technique, which was very compatible to my learning style. For me, this was the true beginning of the journey with Neal and Dr. Laura. They both were providing me with constant challenges and work to stop my eating disorder behaviors and to challenge beliefs that had manifested and strengthened in me over the years. Refeeding my brain and working on these challenges were the keys in helping me to start working toward a much healthier state of mind so I could do the work needed around my trauma.

I finally started to open up a little bit more each time I met with Neal. The work we went through was breaking down the walls of my fear, shame, and anger. It was more work than I ever dreamed. I still felt scared that I needed to protect my secret out of shame, embarrassment, and ongoing pain of the details of the torture I endured. It was Neal who constantly worked on breaking down the myths and my old beliefs. The secret was my pain and suffering. I realized the secret I kept was festering within me, and I needed to let go of the secrets of what happened to me. I found the help I needed to begin to trust in the journey, and I learned about the skill *radical acceptance.*

My journey of healing began when I realized I needed to be more assertive in life. I needed to tell my story, my secrets. I needed to accept what happened and learn to ask for help. This journey I was about to begin was the need to learn how to express myself to others and how to reach for help by letting others know my story. As I looked online for a story like mine, I found a lot of stories of pain and suffering. I instantly wanted to reach out and tell these people that I understood, and that there is a way out of their hell. I so wanted to find these individuals that were so scared; I wanted to reach out and to tell my story so they would know they weren't alone. Many people who are abused don't know that the fear they feel is based on the emotion of shame. I wanted these individuals out there to know their fear was real—but they needed to be assertive, ask for help, and let others know they were hurting. There're so many different ways people feel after being violated, tortured, or degraded. I too remember feeling stuck, ashamed, and unable to tell anyone my story. I lived my life in fear.

When I was taught that shame was my main reaction to being abused, I unfortunately still assumed I needed to keep silent; these were not the things to talk about. Well, that's what I learned, and believed. My fears then became my secrets, my shame. Actually, this belief I had developed just added to my fear. So, not only was I abused, feeling humiliated and degraded; but I then felt that speaking up would just add more shame and fear. It became one ugly circle.

I hated this horrific life experience and I twisted the hate I had for what was done to me, into the hate of myself. This self-hate and poor body image I developed soon became my identity. Something had to change, and I knew I needed to change my thoughts and my beliefs…so I could heal.

As I started to write this book, I realized many others could understand my journey because **trauma** comes in many forms. A traumatic event could be a loss of a loved one, divorce, medical difficulties, natural disasters, rape, abandonment, addiction, domestic abuse…the list goes on. For me, the trauma not only affected me personally, it created a living hell for all those closest to me. It was painful to see how my suffering was also a burden that my husband and children suffered as I fought to survive the pain. The trauma exacerbated my **eating disorder** to new levels. It is difficult to believe how **out of control I was, and how, being so malnourished, my mind actually believed that my eating disorder was what was keeping me in control**. It also created **self-destructive behaviors** and **anxiety** that turned to unbearable **self-hate**. I lost myself into the world of my eating disorder, and all hell broke loose. I found myself **spiraling out of control**, sitting at death's doorstep!

The debilitating eating disorder, and then the unexpected trauma which I experienced, derailed me off my path of life. Those things stripped me of the life that I knew, and instead dealt me the life of fear and anxiety. My new goal was to find health and a life worth living—with the ultimate goal of sharing this story to inspire others to a path of healing.

I wanted this book to be available for those who experienced traumas (of any kind), eating disorders, addictions, and other mental health issues. Also, for those who have experienced and walked in similar paths of pain and suffering, I hope my story will help provide information for them that includes how to find therapists, doctors, dietitians, and social workers who are reaching out to help people like us.

Let the **journey of a life worth living** begin.

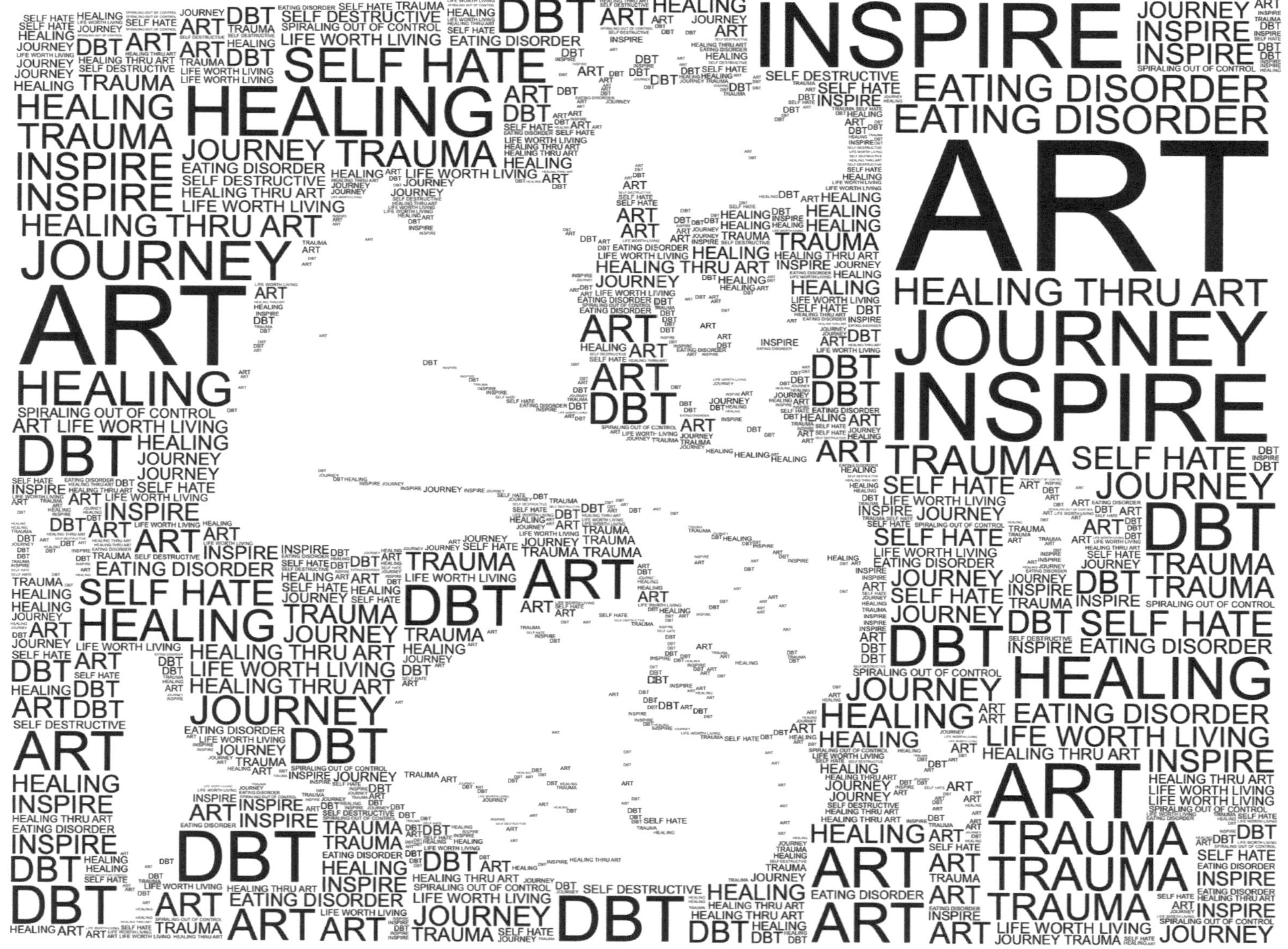

CHAPTER TWO

From a Psychologist's Perspective: My Role in Kathleen's Journey

by Dr. Laura Lees

Throughout my career as a clinical psychologist, I have had the opportunity to work alongside some very talented art therapists. I have witnessed firsthand how Art Therapy can reach people on an emotional level that is different from that of traditional talk therapy. From my perspective, Art Therapy is a tool that helps people express thoughts, feelings or experiences they can't necessarily verbalize. Art provides an opportunity to represent internal perceptions on paper or through other mediums.

When I began working with Kathleen, I quickly learned she was not only an educator, but also an artist and a Registered Art Therapist. When Kathleen began to share her artwork with me, we explored what it meant and represented to her. Although she was so emotionally shut down at the beginning of treatment, her art was something she connected to, and it turned out to be a way I could start showing her the feelings she artistically represented on paper, that she could not yet put into words.

As she brought me her work from years ago up to the present in search for meaning and understanding, we found a common means of connection that allowed us to process her journals and artwork in a way that made sense to her. As she was learning and processing new information and a new self-understanding about her feelings, it was like watching a transformation.

"Art" does not necessarily equate to "artistic" and does not require any creative skill. The value in Art Therapy is in its *process*, not in the final *product*. The finished Art Therapy piece may reflect literal images that we can see, describe, and understand based on the issues the patient is working through in conventional therapy. For example, one of Kathleen's pieces is clearly a face with a teardrop falling from the eye which reflected her shame and sadness.

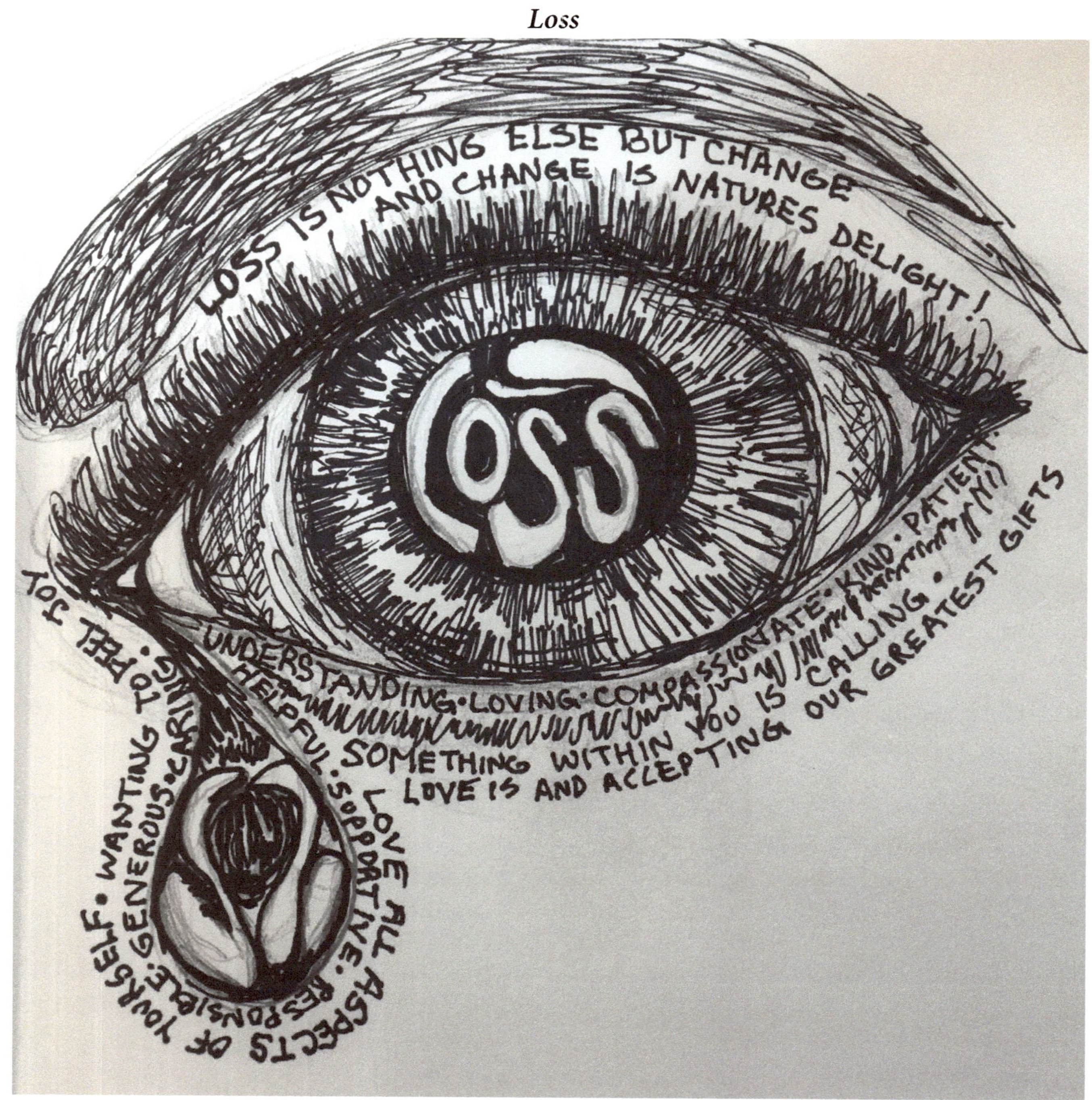
LOSS IS NOTHING ELSE BUT CHANGE
AND CHANGE IS NATURES DELIGHT!
LOSS
UNDERSTANDING • LOVING • COMPASSIONATE • KIND • PATIENT •
HELPFUL • SUPPORTIVE • LOVE ALL ASPECTS OF YOURSELF • WANTING
TO FEEL JOY • GIVING • GENEROUS • CARING • RESPONSIBLE •
SOMETHING WITHIN YOU IS CALLING •
LOVE IS AND ACCEPTING OUR GREATEST GIFTS

An Art Therapy piece can also be abstract, something that only the creator may be able to describe, as their work depicts their inner experience in a form or format that isn't obvious to the person looking at it.

Kathleen liked to paint scenery and people. One day I gave her an assignment to draw her emotions. She was challenged by this because, for years, she denied she had feelings and she wasn't able to cognitively process them, especially anger. What she ended up drawing was a series of circles overlapping and intertwining. It wasn't really thought out that way, which is the point—for this assignment Kathleen had to rely on what she felt instead of what she thought.

The intention was to help her acknowledge and express the feelings she wasn't even aware she had. This is what she painted:

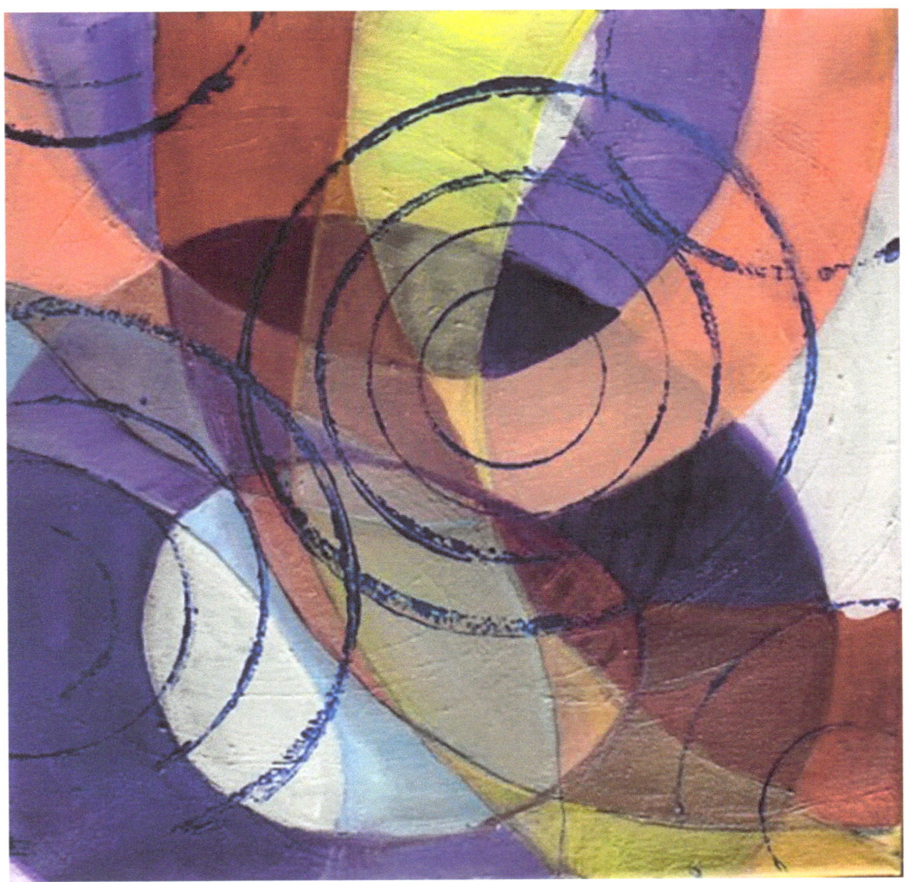

The circles were linking and represented her confusion and her inability to figure out what her feelings were. This confusion was reflected on paper through color and texture, along with the complexity of layering and interlocking the circles. As she worked through the process, Kathleen struggled with how to decipher which circle, representing a feeling, should be in front and which should be behind. A seemingly simple assignment became very complicated for her because she tried to intellectualize it too much—she just needed to "feel the feels."

Whether a person is given a directive to work on something specific or just chooses to create on their own, Art Therapy is meant to be an organic process. When my patients show me their art, because I know their personalities and the therapeutic issues they are working through, I can usually make some interpretations of the artwork. Now, those are just *my* interpretations, which doesn't necessarily make them correct, but they may provide some insights into what the art represents. More importantly, the patient's interpretations of their thoughts, feelings and experiences are what can help them progress in their recovery.

In Kathleen's case, she often just draws or creates art on her own and, while it may look like one thing on the surface, knowing her background and what else she is working on in therapy, we are able to expand upon the interpretation of what may appear obvious. For example, her drawing of the woman and child is just that…on the surface. But, knowing Kathleen's trauma history, the child could represent a number of different things, such as abuse that took place, the need for nurturing, the feeling of neglect, or it may represent the inner part of her, sometimes referred to as the child that still exists within the adult.

At a time when she was really struggling with body image, Kathleen brought in a set of pictures she drew many years ago that represented her anorexic body: starved, very worn out, and fragile looking. Even though they showed what her physical body looked like many years ago, in the present they represent her internal body image—what she sees in her mind's eye.

So, while Kathleen's every thought and behavior was still fully anorexic in nature, with weight gain, her body soon became her most horrid and ghastly nightmare. She felt "desperate and panicky" to do something about her weight but no amount of restricting or exercising was having any effect. Her art expressed the confusion over what her body looked like then versus what she sees now. This discrepancy created a battle within as she struggled to let go of self-loathing and find peace with her body as it is. The art provided a visual of the difference between her actual body and her internal representation of it.

Kathleen still struggles with body image, but when she was starved and weak and frail, she could not *see* herself accurately. All she saw was fat. Part of the reason for this is explained by the process of starvation and what it does to the brain. Not only is the body starved and significantly underweight, the brain atrophies (shrinks) as a result of starvation. Weight loss also results in the loss of brain mass and it is estimated that losing five pounds is equivalent to losing millions of brain cells.

Important parts of the brain are affected, such as the visual and spatial areas that allow us to "see" ourselves with our eyes closed or when it's not possible to look in a mirror. This is the part of the brain where our internal body image, or how we see ourselves in our mind's eye, is located. Research has been conducted using neuroimaging which shows certain parts of the brain that regulate body image don't light up in those with anorexia, while other parts that regulate fear are overactive. When the brain's anatomy shrinks, blood flow to important areas is reduced and this too can affect the way someone perceives their body shape and size.

At a time when Kathleen was in a severe anorexic state, she went through a stage where her drawings were all black and white. Her brain was so severely malnourished that she was unable to see color and, in a strange way, her entire life turned to black and white. Not only was her brain unable to process color, the quality of her art noticeably declined and became regressive. Looking at her art at her lowest weight and then her art as her weight improved, there is a *striking* difference. The former looks as if it was drawn by a child while the latter clearly looks like it was created by someone with notable artistic skill.

I encourage all my patients to use art of any kind to express their thoughts and feelings because it is an excellent coping skill. Some really like it, but it's not for everyone. I believe it is the therapist's responsibility to figure out what strategies and interventions work for each patient and that it's critical to individualize each person's therapy by finding a range of tools and skills that the patient benefits from.

I generally categorize coping skills into two types. One type is called **distractor coping** and the other is called **process coping**. For those who have trouble dealing with emotions, or at times when a break from feelings or engaging in unhealthy behaviors is needed, distracting oneself by watching a television show, calling a friend, or playing a game on the phone can be very helpful. Art is another way to distract and get relief from feelings or behaviors.

While distractor coping is very effective, it isn't healthy to only distract. Feelings also need to be attended to, and process coping skills are a way to do that. With this type of coping, feelings are actively being dealt with in some way, such as talking to someone about the feeling, writing or journaling about it, or using art to visually express the feeling.

Kathleen has learned to use art for both distraction and process coping. Whether it is doodling to distract or combining journaling with drawing to actively process, creating art brings her into a mindful state. It's a grounding strategy that brings her into the present moment at times when feelings are overwhelming or thoughts spin into catastrophizing.

People with eating disorders are often thinking way out into the future or back into the past and are therefore not living in the present. Focusing on the paper, the colors, the textures, and the image right in front of her helps Kathleen bring herself into the now. In that way it can serve as a distractor that gets her out of dysfunctional thinking about the future and the past. The assignment I gave her to draw her feelings was a way for her to process emotions by choosing shapes and colors to represent what she didn't have words for. Then, we processed the art together in session which helped to make sense out of the image on a different emotional level. We both had interpretations of the piece that gave Kathleen insight into specific feelings and why she was having them.

When I first met Kathleen, she had been eating about 25% of a normal daily intake for many years, and the few foods she would eat were not providing much nutrition at all. At the time, she was so numbed out by chronic starvation that she's what I refer to as a "walking head"—she had no access to her feelings as if there were no connection between her body and her mind. It was as if her head and her body weren't even attached, that's how cognitively and emotionally cut off she presented.

Eating disordered behaviors starve the body and brain of nutrition and, as a result, they end up numbing out feelings. When the brain is starved, it atrophies, or shrinks in size, and the neurotransmitters, or brain chemicals that regulate mood, are disrupted. Over time, one of the functions an eating disorder serves is to block out feelings that are too difficult to tolerate. Kathleen had experienced severe trauma as an adult and her eating disorder served the purpose of keeping her numbed out from having feelings or thinking about the trauma that was haunting her.

Generally, eating disorders are not caused by societal messages extolling the virtues of thinness. However, a person who has the genetic predisposition to an eating disorder is going to be much more sensitive to societal pressures, the influences of social and other types of media, and messages they receive in their personal environment (family, school, work, extracurricular activities, etc.). Those elements are like magnets and are easy to get caught up in when the predisposition exists. An initial goal to "eat healthy" or to go on a diet can morph into an out of control eating disorder in no time.

Those who do not have the genetic predisposition are either less susceptible to those pressures or, when they decide to "eat healthy," it tends to be more transitory. They go on the diet and then they go off the diet; it doesn't morph into an eating disorder. That's why an estimated 45 million people diet every year but only about 8 million of them develop an eating disorder.

In Kathleen's case, trauma and anxiety were the triggers to the initiation of her eating disorder in her early teenage years; then severe trauma as an adult significantly exacerbated it. Anorexia, bingeing and purging, and excessive exercise led her to the point where she literally couldn't function. In fact, she ended up on the verge of death, in a coma, and on a ventilator for a month due to aspiration pneumonia—a severe infection that developed when vomit entered her lungs.

When Kathleen and I started working together and she was in the "walking head" phase, I would talk about feelings and she would look at me like I had three eyes. She would proudly say, "I don't have feelings," as though that were a badge of honor. The ironic thing was, she exuded anger and had no idea. She tried to convince me, "I'm not angry. I don't have anything to be angry about," all the while taking it out on herself and on her body.

Starving, purging, and excessively exercising were ways she was taking anger out on herself. She was actively abusing herself in order to avoid facing the sexual abuse that was committed against her.

Kathleen was so emotionally numb that she would engage in self-harm by cutting herself. The intent of the self-harm was not to end her life. She was searching for feeling. All of the feelings she had about the trauma that she couldn't allow into her conscious awareness, express verbally, or experience otherwise were being acted out on her body. Eating disorder behaviors and self-harm were the physical manifestations and expressions of feelings that she couldn't process internally or make sense of in her head. The physical pain was the only feeling she could tolerate and it served two purposes—one was to feel *something* physically, the other was to feel *nothing* emotionally.

So, she numbed herself out, but not intentionally. No one plans or decides to get an eating disorder and no one knows that an eating disorder eventually becomes a form of coping. Anytime Kathleen would start to feel emotions associated with the trauma, she would immediately turn to eating disorder behaviors to block out those feelings. She didn't want to think or feel anything about the trauma so she focused on self-hate and self-blame and punished herself by causing physical destruction and pain. The physical pain was easier to handle than the emotional pain.

The more weight Kathleen lost, the more her cognitive functioning suffered and the more obsessive-compulsive she became. She created so many rules that there was barely any food, in any amount, that was permissible to eat. Food had to be cut a certain way. Her dietitian explained how during one point of Kathleen's eating disorder, she created a rule in her head that at every meal she sat down to, she had to have a peach cut into the shape of a flower on her plate which she believed was the only way she could eat the meal in front of her. Obsessive-compulsive behaviors always ruled her eating: counting how many times she would chew a bite of food; not having food groups touching each other on the plate, excessively organizing everything on the table, including salt, pepper, silverware, cups, and glasses, before she would eat—the rules were never ending. Breaking any of them equated to being "bad," and the only answer to that was punishing herself in one of a variety of ways.

Because of severe and chronic malnutrition, Kathleen was not able to think clearly or logically in therapy sessions. She would automatically twist my words; for example, when I talked about the importance of dietary fat, she would respond "If I eat more fat, I'm just going to get fatter. I'm already fat, how can I eat more fat?" She wasn't able to process educational information about the need for fat along with protein and carbohydrates, and that by increasing calories it was possible to increase metabolism. All she could hear was the word "FAT." The rest of the message was lost and resulted in her automatic conclusion: "I am going to *get fatter.*"

Another message that Kathleen twisted was compliments. If I complimented her outfit or a new haircut, she twisted that into believing I was looking at her fat and all I saw was how disgusting and ugly she was. She was by far her own worst enemy. Her eating disorder beliefs were working against her and amplified her fear of fat and her fear of gaining weight.

The fear of fat and weight gain can serve to simplify things for people with complicated trauma histories and experiences. It's much easier to be afraid of getting fat than it is to face the actual fears and pain that underlie trauma. When the focus is kept on the fear of getting fat, it provides an illusion of control—that something can be done about that fear immediately—starving, purging, exercising—something can be done *right now* to deal with that fear and to control weight. There is nothing easy about dealing with the compound fear attached to trauma; but that fear is the very thing that causes people to feel out of control. The fear of fat is a forceful distractor that deceptively keeps everything simple.

Another method of distraction was exercise. When Kathleen felt any kind of anxiety, she would immediately go to the gym—sometimes three or four times a day—and focus on burning off fat. People at the gym would see her there all the time and compliment her on her drive and commitment, observing that she was losing weight. That only compelled her to do it more which reinforced the eating disorder. Her behavior was misinterpreted as being driven, disciplined, and dedicated—but it was actually obligatory, compulsive, and destructive.

For many years Kathleen was controlled by the number on the scale. She would step on and off of it multiple times every morning, hoping the number would change and go down between steps. Early in treatment, I asked her to bring her scale to me. She went white as a ghost at that request. I was asking her to give up some control and she (actually, the eating disorder) didn't like it at all.

Getting on the scale every morning determined what kind of day Kathleen would have. She literally didn't know what to do without it. She reluctantly brought her scale in one day after weighing herself multiple times in the parking lot of my office, out where anyone could have seen her. Although she left the scale with me, the same day she went out and bought another one. The illusion of having control by knowing the number is very compelling.

I eventually learned that Kathleen also kept a scale in her car. Her anxiety was so high all the time that checking her weight on demand, no matter where she went, was the factor she used to determine if she needed to go to the gym and/ or purge. The number was never right and the eating disorder was always the answer to feeling fat and disgusting. As is the case with the compulsive nature of eating disorder behaviors, Kathleen, who worked tirelessly not to feel anything, kept herself preoccupied by focusing on her weight, feeling fat, excessively exercising, and starving and purging, so there was no time or space to think about anything else.

The purging became excessive, occurring numerous times per day. It was doing physical harm to her body and was exhausting. Even though Kathleen knew this, she didn't try to stop purging. Instead, she took her phone into the bathroom with her in case something happened and she needed to call 911. It never occurred to her that it might be too late to make the call.

She was hospitalized on numerous occasions, and many of those times, required a feeding tube that was inserted through her nose and down into her stomach in order to supply a liquid nutritional supplement. Despite the feeding tube, she would continue to purge and the tube would come out of her stomach and into her mouth. She didn't want the hospital staff to know she did this, so instead of having a nurse reinsert the tube, she would do it herself. This was very dangerous and it led to multiple cases of aspiration pneumonia. Four of the episodes were so severe that Kathleen fell into a coma. The last time, she was in a coma for a month and was not expected to survive.

Within the field of eating disorders, one of the first goals of treatment is to "rescue the brain" because starvation and malnutrition negatively affect important brain functions. The brain actually atrophies or shrinks, and the neurotransmitters, or the chemicals that regulate thinking, feeling, and behavior, are all significantly affected. Until the brain starts functioning again, the ability to think clearly, make more rational decisions, use better judgment, gain access to feelings, and begin to improve, coping remains impaired. A malnourished body and brain result in that "walking head" state which prevents meaningful therapeutic work from occurring.

The brain needs to be renourished so that the head and body can realign, allowing for the ability to emotionally process feelings and issues. Otherwise, just talking about them while being detached from them is like telling someone else's story. Kathleen was in therapy for many years before I met her and hadn't received the treatment she needed to rescue her brain. Consequently, she was too numb and too invested in the eating disorder as a way to punish and distract herself; so, sadly, no progress toward her eating disorder recovery was made.

Since Neal and I have been working with Kathleen, her improvement has been remarkable. She is a completely different person than the "walking head" I first met. She's emotionally connected—she has feelings and openly admits them and shows them! After A LOT of very hard work to face huge fears about eating without purging, she can now come to session and say that she is angry. She can cry. She can talk about feelings and stressors without purging or cutting or starving.

She had to face her fears of eating, her fears of weight gain and her fear of being out of control with food. Her meal plan was broken down and became an important part of her daily DBT Diary Card that both Neal and I reviewed at each session. Without rescuing the brain, she would not have been able to learn the DBT skills that showed her she can tolerate the memories and feelings she was convinced would literally kill her if she ever let them out.

CHAPTER THREE

The Function of an Eating Disorder

Working with Dr. Laura, I was building an understanding how the development of an eating disorder can begin early in life, and how it also can creep up on a person. The eating disorder can—and often does—start even before the person realizes there is a problem. For me (and many other individuals who have an eating disorder), there exists what is called a predisposition. Do note that not everyone with these predisposition markers ends up with an eating disorder. Many of us who do develop eating disorders have poor self-worth and are perfectionists; and possibly deal with some form of depression, obsessive compulsive disorders, and poor emotion-regulation skills. The important aspect to understand is that the eating disorder serves as an important function. Eating disorders don't just appear, they develop—with great purpose—even if unconscious to the individual.

You may ask, *what could you possibly mean—the eating disorder has a purpose?* Yes, it absolutely does. This complex illness develops unintentionally, but fiercely, over time, beginning as a functional coping mechanism for the individual.

While the illness is debilitating mentally, emotionally, and physically in the long run, understanding the function of the eating disorder can help those who struggle with it to replace this function with a sustainable, healthier coping mechanism. This helps their families as well!

Understanding the function behind the eating disorder can enhance recovery by:

- noticing the function of eating disorder behaviors is designed to numb or to cope

- increasing awareness of symptoms: No one chooses this illness!

- increasing awareness surrounding the triggers for the development of the illness

- connecting to, and learning how to ask for, what you need

- replacing the function of the eating disorder with healthier coping mechanisms

I already had signs of an eating disorder before adolescence. My parents said they recognized bizarre eating at an early stage in my life. Back then, eating disorders were not common or well known. When a person who is predisposed to an eating disorder adds trauma, the function of the eating disorder becomes the coping mechanism.

Dr. Laura noticed that, when I brought in my journals and artwork, they were not only a tool for communication, but a stored timeline. I also realized when I brought in my artwork and gave an unspoken tool that helped me to build on trust and the relationship I needed to have with her as I was opening up more and understanding what my paintings kept, as I silently was screaming for help. The trust I built with Dr. Laura, along with the help of my art skills, and determination to get better, drove my desire to push forward to learn both the skills needed, and how to break the hold of the eating disorder. I had to believe that, with all these pieces in place, I could find my voice and break free from old behaviors and the relentless eating disorder which was trying to destroy me.

I shared my artwork during my sessions with Dr. Laura. We spoke about how I felt and about the feelings represented in my artwork. Interestingly, we discovered my artwork was my only way to communicate my pain, and consequently was drawn during a period of time when women were never heard or validated. Just recently there has been progress—thanks to groups like "Me Too"—for abused and assaulted women to find a voice to bring justice and closure.

Dr. Laura not only helped me with finding my voice, but showed me the value of my artwork and how years of my drawings, paintings and journal doodles were useful for us in building a bond and an avenue of communication. Dr. Laura and I were then ready to work together to understand how to break the hold of my eating disorder.

I'm going to let the words of this sketching/painting speak for themselves. It doesn't matter what your trauma might be; there are so many traumatic events that destroy lives. As I walked my journey, I wanted to wrap my arms around the many individuals who experienced their own trauma. I

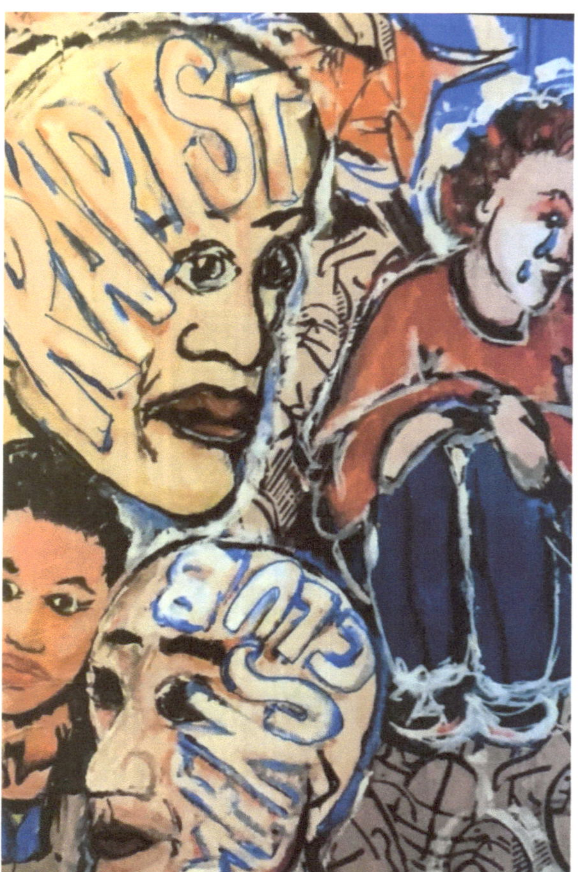

Giving Your Trauma a Voice!

wanted to show those who suffer that there is hope. I want to help individuals like myself to find their own path to healing by sharing my story. Remember, our experiences don't define us and don't have to become our identity. We don't have to lose our identity. It is a part of our life's experience. It is what we do with it that defines us, *that* is who we are.

During the darkest days of my eating disorder, there were no words that could describe the pain, the suffering, or the humiliation I went through. It created a hole within me that filled with shame, loneliness, despair, and self-hatred. It is the most daunting pain, and I had no control over it. With help I finally could understand and grasp that the guilt is not mine to carry.

These were some of the darkest days, where I neared what I thought was the only way out.

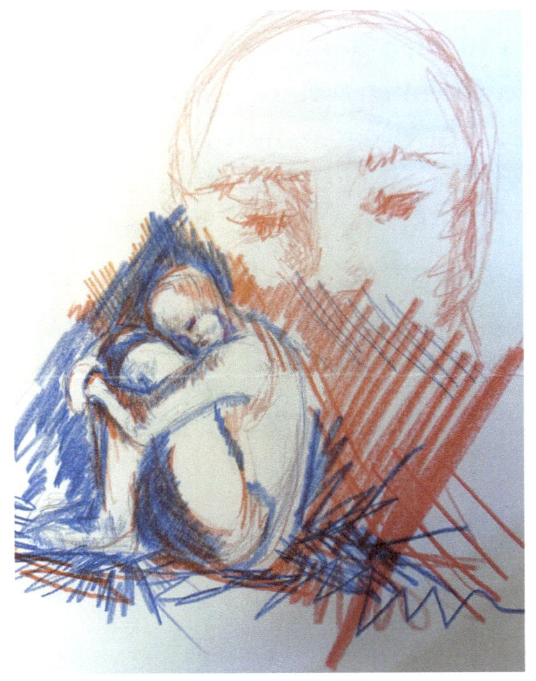 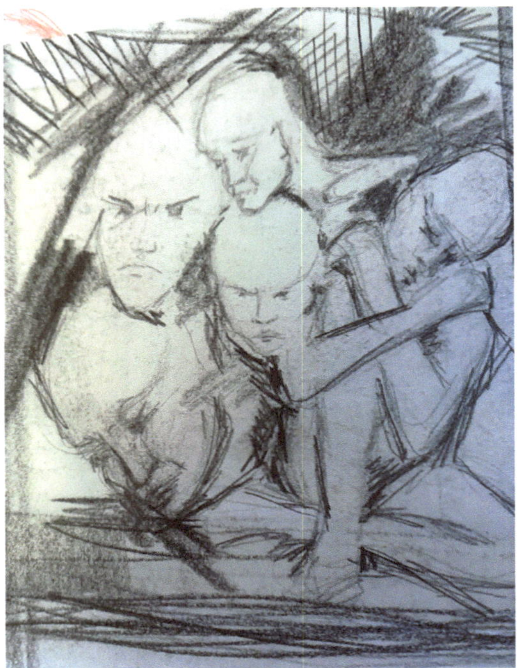

I found these two pencil sketches in my journals. They were from back in my "black-and-white series." These are reflective of my life living in a dark black hole. I was identified as one of the revolving door patients: my eating disorder was destroying me, and I was in and out of the hospital, making progress and then relapsing. My health deteriorated so much I was hospitalized multiple times. With all these hospitalizations, what I didn't connect to was just how much the trauma I experienced really had such a big effect on me. I believe now that this was the reason I continually ended up in the hospital. I was too sick and numb from both the effects of the eating disorder and the additional effects from the trauma.

Now I can look back and see how the two connected. The eating disorder unconsciously kept me numb and focused on food, not reality. It was much easier to focus on food rather than what was really the issue, which was the fear of my memories and the trauma I experienced. The trauma was so intense it circled back to needing the eating disorder to avoid feeling the pain and suffering. Ultimately the trauma was horrific, but it was my inability to deal with the feelings and hiding behind my eating disorder that was destroying me.

It is so common for many women like me to turn inward to guilt and self-hate. I was a young woman who had no skills or cognition to cope in a more effective way. Over the years I began to have an understanding of the purpose of, and reasons for, why we have our emotions. These emotions do have a purpose; they motivate us to solve problems and learn from them. Initially, I struggled with connecting to my feelings. What I knew growing up was to please people, have a smile on my face, and be determined and successful. I didn't realize the importance of identifying with my emotions. Surprisingly enough, my artwork did. I was screaming out for help in each of my sketches. I wanted to tell my story, and my artwork, at the time, was the only words I had. Everything was secret, which only built more shame within me. I lived in fear, and I felt if anyone knew my story it would fall on deaf ears—I would be rejected and labeled a defect. It boiled down to ill-stated beliefs that I had created long before. Those beliefs kept me in self-hate and kept me feeling that I was a failure if anyone knew the truth of what happened to me and the fact that I had an eating disorder for the majority of my life.

My sketches often connected to my pain, but they were doodles that I had kept private in my journals. They were for no one to see. I didn't realize the importance of my drawings or even my doodles. Later, I realized my drawings were my outlet—my true expression of my emotions

It was at this time my eating disorder was in full control. This dark period of my life was ruled by denial—I could not see what was obvious to others. I felt chained to this eating disorder; it felt like there was no way out. It was destroying me. I was so willful, I refused to make choices to correct my unhealthy life.

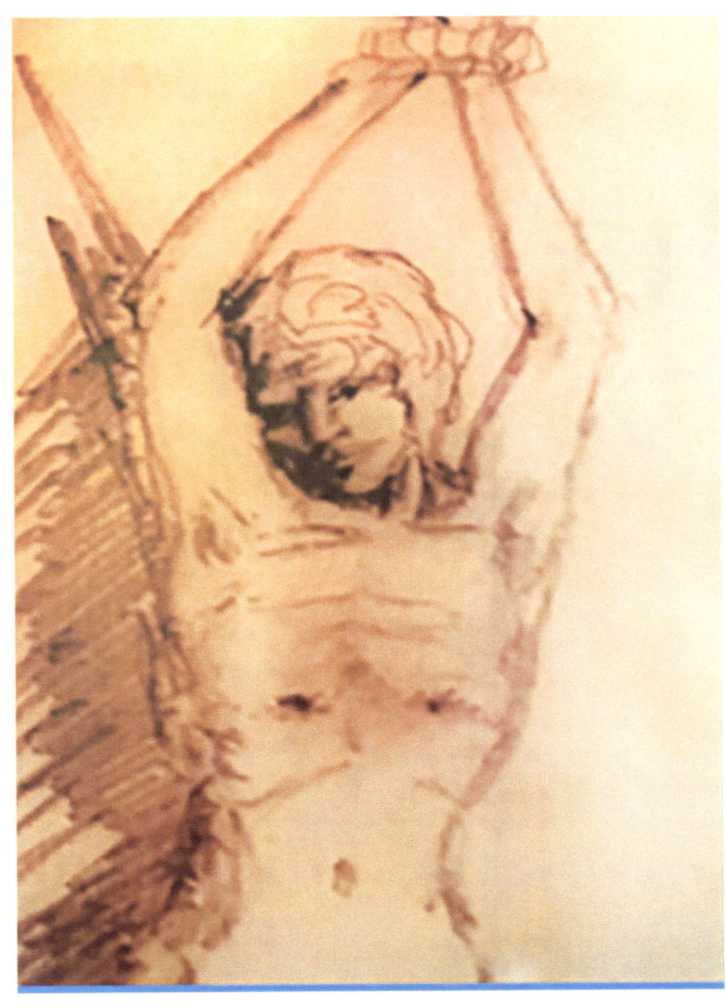

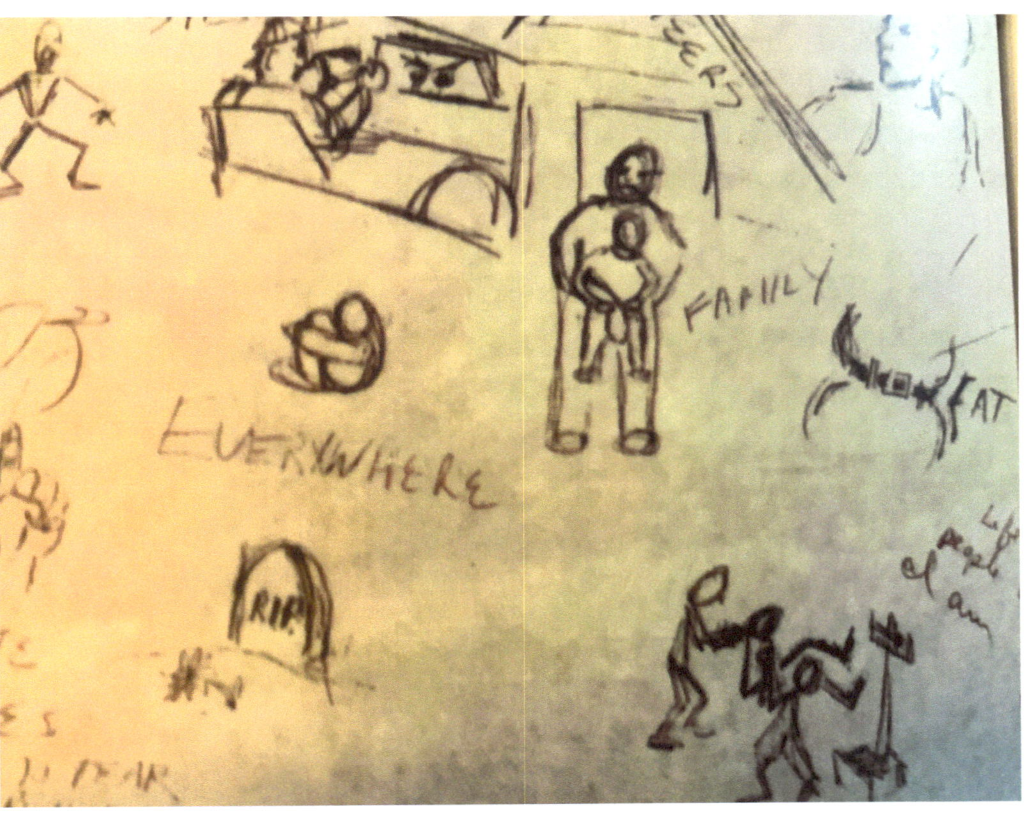
FAMILY
EVERYWHERE
EAT
RIP

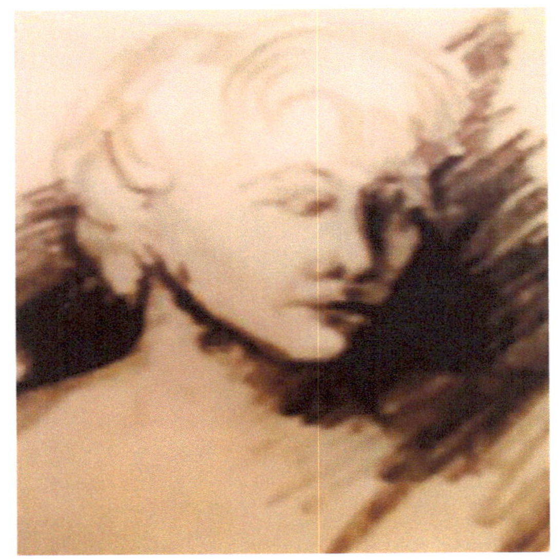

I remained stuck in this black-and-white format of sketching during this regressive stage of my life. I now know that my eating disorder was so profound and debilitating, it stole the gift I was given from birth: the ability to see color and draw. I was born to be an artist, expressing life with vibrant colors. When I was so underweight, I lost the ability to see and experience the vibrant colors of life all around me.

I drew many pictures like these in my journals. Unfortunately, I threw out many journals over the years, thinking I was protecting myself and my family. I figured if no one read my thoughts during that time, no one would know. I didn't realize at the time that many of my drawings were so regressive, but they were the only way I knew how to scream for help.

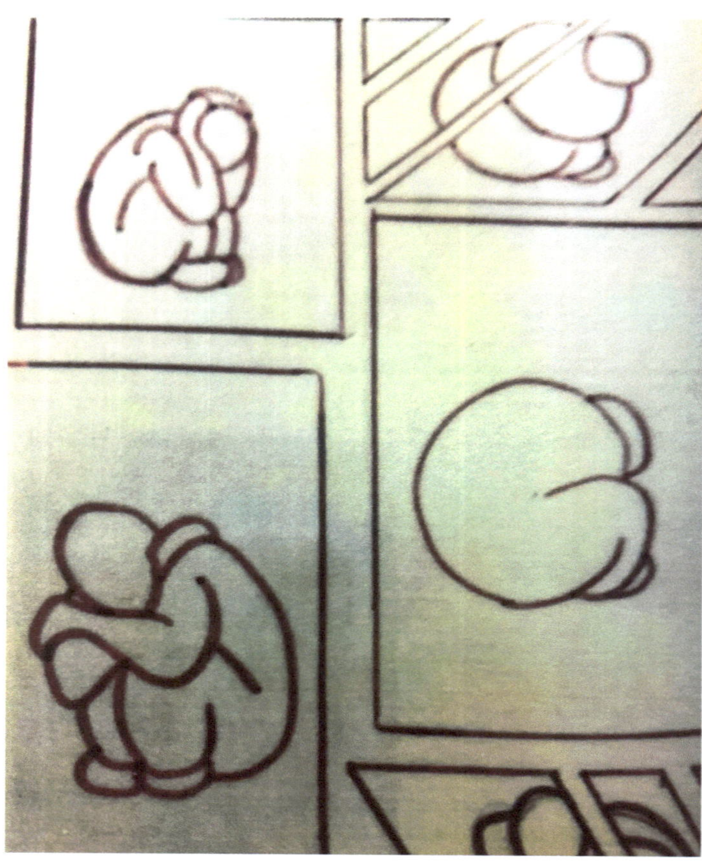

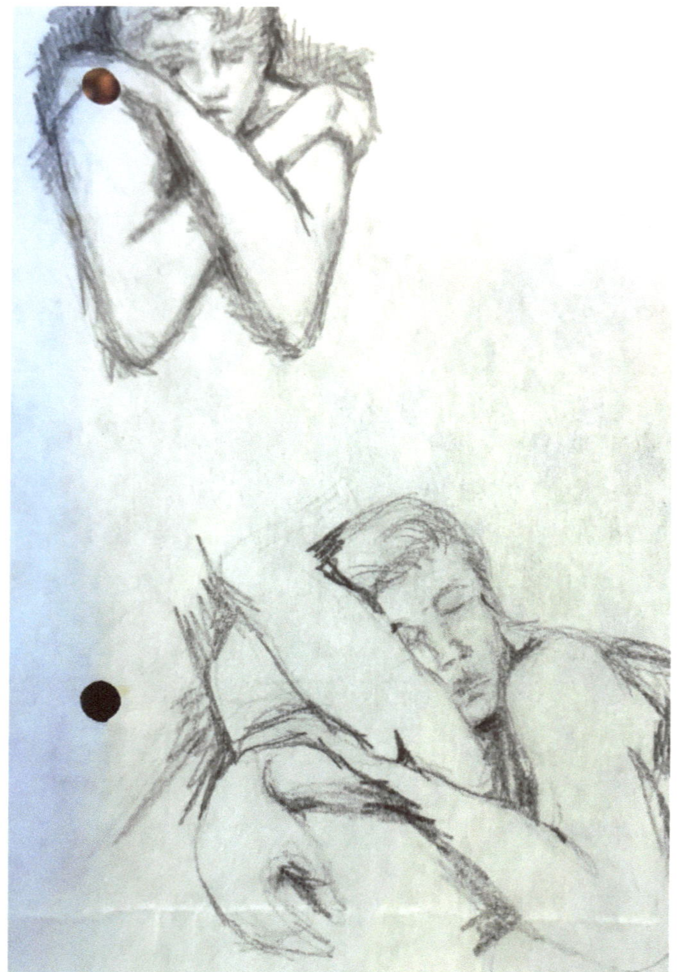

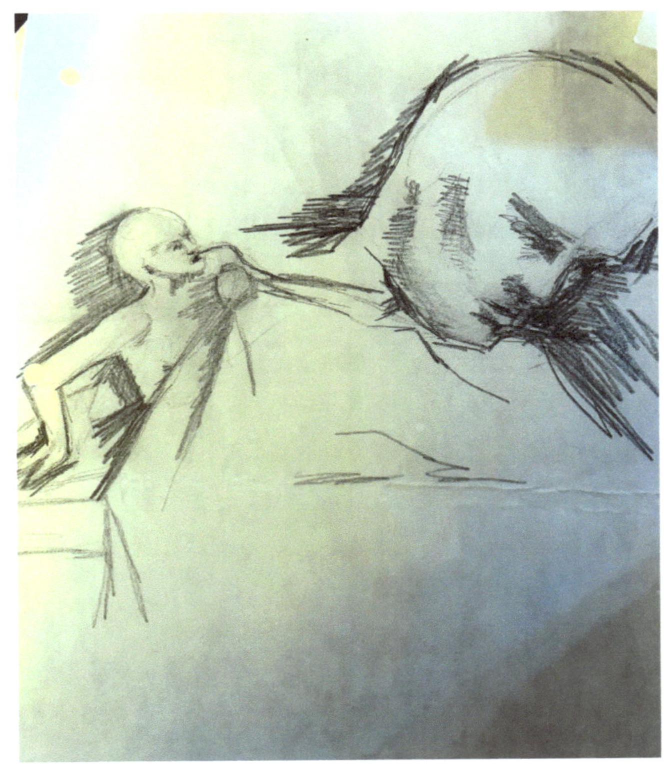

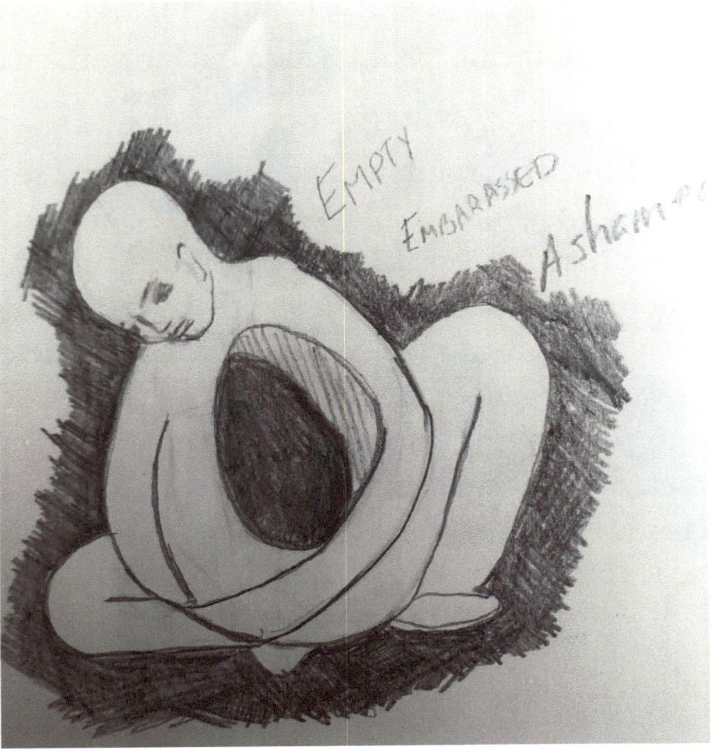

It was not until I began to work through what they called the "refeeding process," which was adding vital nutrients to refuel my body and brain, that I got the nourishment I needed to function. As I began to refeed, and my weight was healthier, I began to see color again. **It was as if a light switch was flipped on.**

What happened to me was morally reprehensible and kept me in a life of fear. Later I learned that besides fear, I was also connecting to shame, anger, and sadness. All of these feelings, that were buried for so long, were now fueled by my eating disorder-thinking. The eating disorder kept my mind preoccupied with non-relevant things. My eating disorder kept me from building an understanding of what happened to me and why I was so numb from the world of reality. The eating disorder created negative thoughts and beliefs that ruled my life. I didn't have the skills I needed to help me to identify with what I was feeling and to get out of hell.

I feared life so much and was so sick, I didn't mind being put in the hospital. At least that's what I thought. Once in the hospital, I wanted out as fast as I got in. I found I wasn't safe in either place. Out of the hospital, I had to deal with the reality of life. In the hospital I had to deal with the reality that I had an eating disorder and to face my trauma.

I remember dreading every day in the hospital when I would stand in line with the other individuals that were also in the eating disorders program. Standing at the nurses' station, wrapped in nothing but a hospital gown, waiting to get our morning weight. Each of us would take our turn stepping up on the scale. We would have to turn our backs, in order to not see the numbers on the scale. We were all panicking as we were waiting our turn. Nearly every one of us still would ask if our weight was up or down that day, but we were met with no response. After being hospitalized so many times, or even just going to the doctor's office, I was determined not to let anyone know my weight, see my weight, or weigh me. I was so afraid of the silent ridicule; I believed everyone was talking about how fat I was. My eating disorder was so strong; the drawing below represents how the number on the scale affected me. I felt like the doctors and hospital staff were determined to punish me by never letting me know the number on the scale. In my head, I was determined to never let anyone get my weight, never to get that number. If they wanted it so badly, they would have to wait until the eating disorder destroyed me and took my life—then they could have my weight.

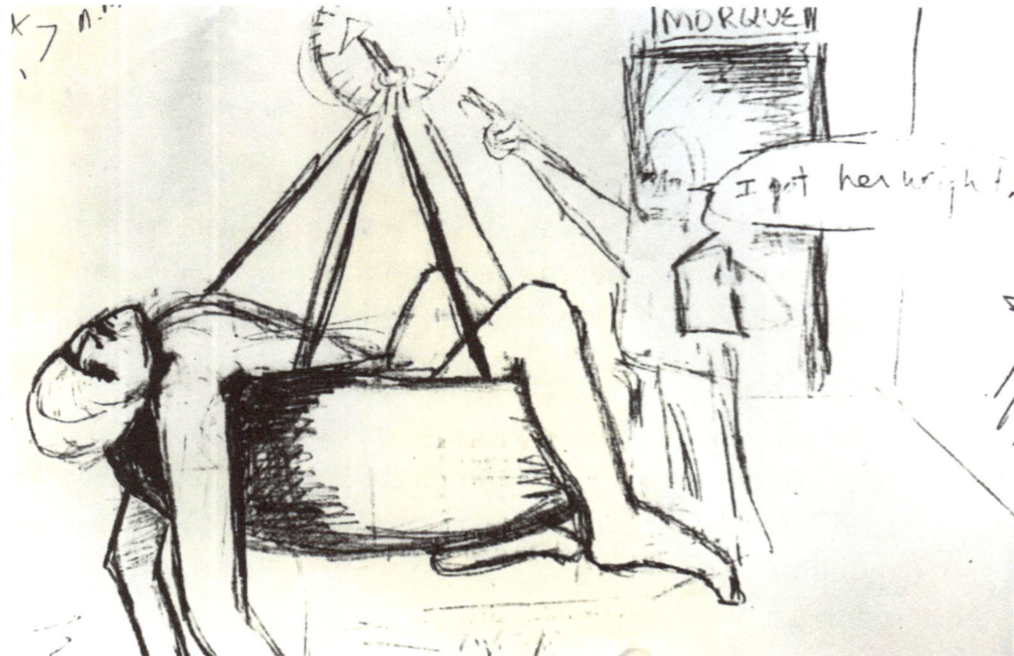

Final Weight

That is how powerful an eating disorder can be, and how distrustful and illogical the thoughts were—and they truly were—running wild in my head.

THE DREADED SCALE!!!!!!!

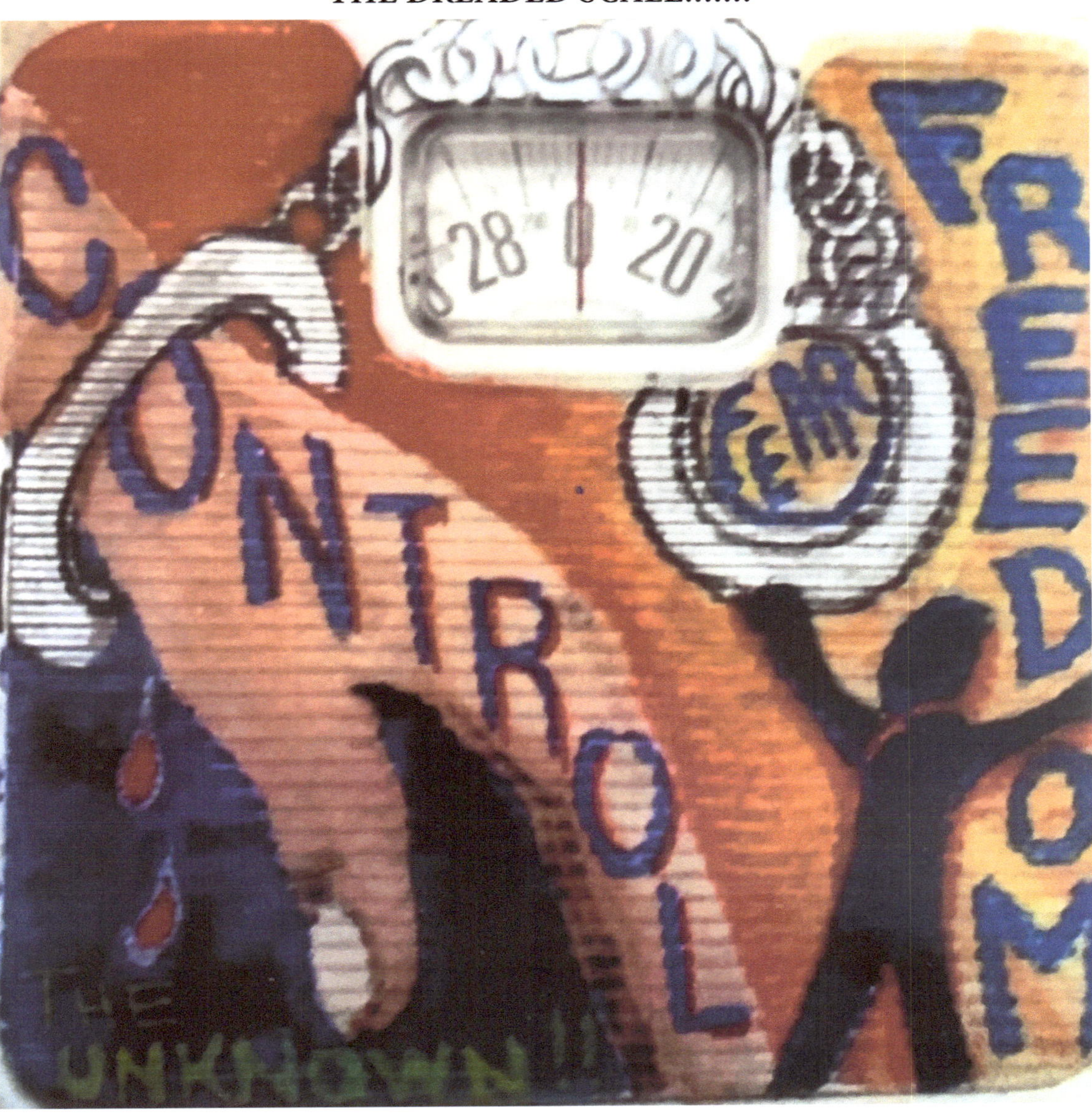

The painting on the scale represents my nemesis. I had a long-standing rivalry with the scale, not just daily, but many, *many* times a day. I turned to the number on the scale as my parameter. Every morning I would wake up to check if I was going to be successful or not that day by standing on the scale. My downfall was I believed that this scale had inescapable powers. It had the ability to decide the fate of each day based on what number it landed on. It ruled my life; it controlled if I was going to have a good day, if I was going out with friends; it even ruled if I was going to go to a planned event or party. This scale had immeasurable power over me. When Dr. Laura had the audacity to demand I hand in my scale, my gut reaction was, *HELL NO!* Although I eventually realized she was correct and I needed to step away from the scale, I felt like a drowning person being asked to let go of a lifeline. After wrestling with my alter egos, I finally brought that scale in and turned it over to her. I complied—technically—but with a little bit of an attitude. I painted the scale to reflect my torment and the misery from it, yet desperately, I could not easily part with it. This painting represents the love/hate relationship I had with the wicked scale. It demonstrates that I was chained to the numbers, that I was *controlled* by the numbers. It was very hard and painful to leave my scale with Dr. Laura, but I could see it brought me freedom. This painting was the *actual scale I had to hand in. It was my painting, with an attitude.*

It was so hard to hand in the scale. It had so much power, I found myself buying more and more scales. My constant need to buy a scale should have been a sign of how out of touch with reality I was. It was more obvious to others that my eating disorder had a lot more of a hold on me, and the sheer madness I was in. I just wasn't seeing it. I felt I needed that scale because it would help make the decisions for me: What I would wear for the day, how many outfits would it take for me to accept what the scale told me, what I could do, and what I could not. Everything was riding on the scale. I had no idea that my buying scale after scale *was* my eating disorder. The bottom line was control; and the rules I made. I needed that scale to stay in control. That was my real thought.

I knew it would create a sense of embarrassment if people knew how much I depended on the number on the scale. But to admit that the scale had control over me? No way. I might have been stubborn by buying five scales, but at that time I strongly believed that there was no connection to me, the scale, and the possibility that the scale represented that the eating disorder was winning.

After my husband watched me continually suffer each day with the dreaded scale, he would ask, "WHY? Why do you continually get yourself so upset by continually getting on the scale?" It made no sense to him. My husband and his friend took it into their own hands to end the misery. They took pictures as they smashed my scale with a sledgehammer. They saw this as a FIX to the problem in their own way. Little did they know, I had to take this step on my own terms, when I had a better grasp of reality.

Death of the Scale!

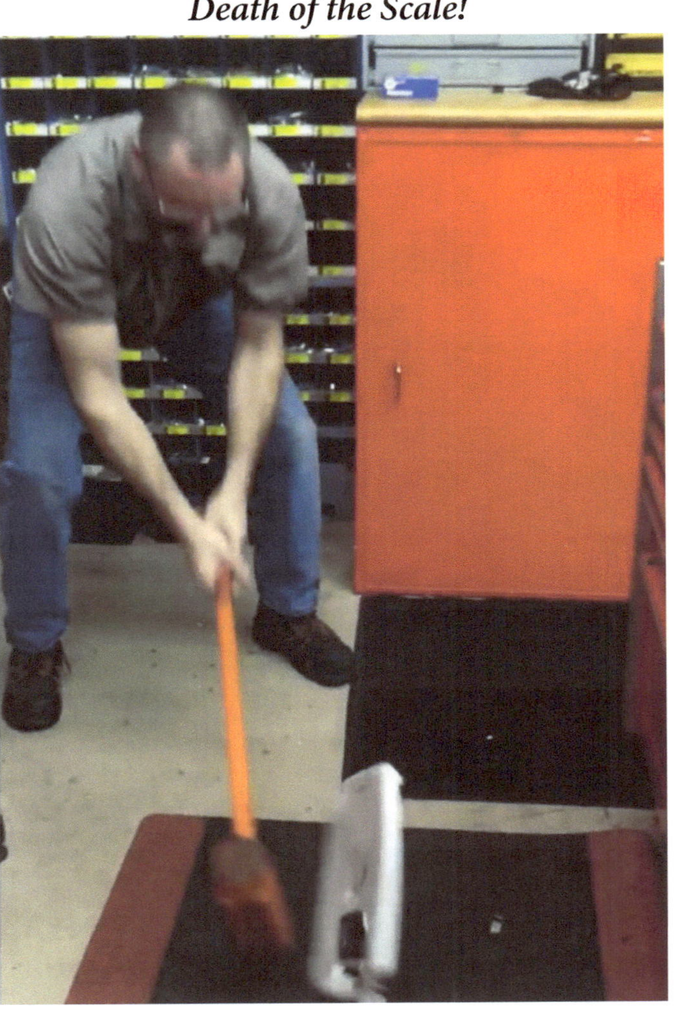

This cartoon was of an office visit to a previous doctor, whom I no longer see. He was determined to get me on the scale, which would decide if I needed another feeding tube inserted. We disagreed on a few things…his view was that "the elephant in the room" was serious; my view was that I had no eating disorder, and I wasn't getting on a scale!

The Elephant in the Room

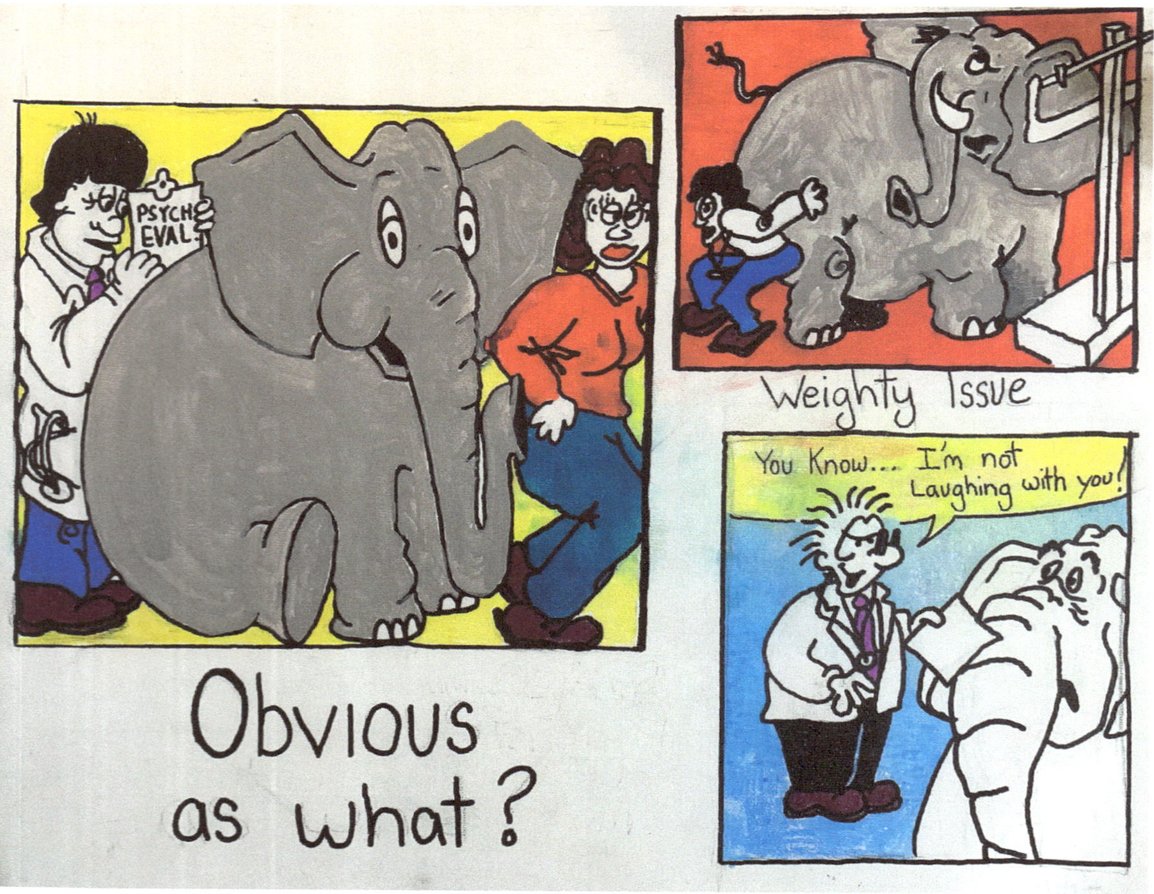

I am working on the reality that the scale does not define me or anything that I do. I am a strong woman who is passionate about her family and about her work helping others. Nowhere on that scale did it read that. The scale is just numbers—data for possible medical use. But by no means does it define me.

CHAPTER FOUR

The Power of Art Therapy

Art Therapy has been defined as a technique used to treat the many needs of individuals with physical and mental health issues. It is based on utilizing the creative art process to express emotions, to develop self-acceptance and personal insight, and, an avenue to healthy choices. As a Registered Art Therapist, I found that my experience has helped many individuals. More recently, I have found that the creative process has given me the hope I needed, and a technique that embraced me as I found a life worth living.

Art Therapy involves a variety of creative outlets, such as sketching, coloring, painting, sculpting, and other art forms, which can be a great help to many clients to express themselves. For many clients, using Art Therapy alongside a credentialed Art Therapist is an opportunity to learn to express themselves through the visual arts when words may not come easily. The work with the Art Therapist provides the clients with an avenue to find a better understanding of the symbolism, metaphors, and other non-verbal messages that are created within the art process.

Art Therapy also helps clients to be more mindful. For me, the art was so self-soothing, I would get lost in my work. I painted the watercolor, shown here, while in the hospital when I needed an outlet to find some form of a mindfulness activity. It was like meditation. It brought me a sense of self soothing and an avenue to feel at ease as I worked on grounding myself. I was

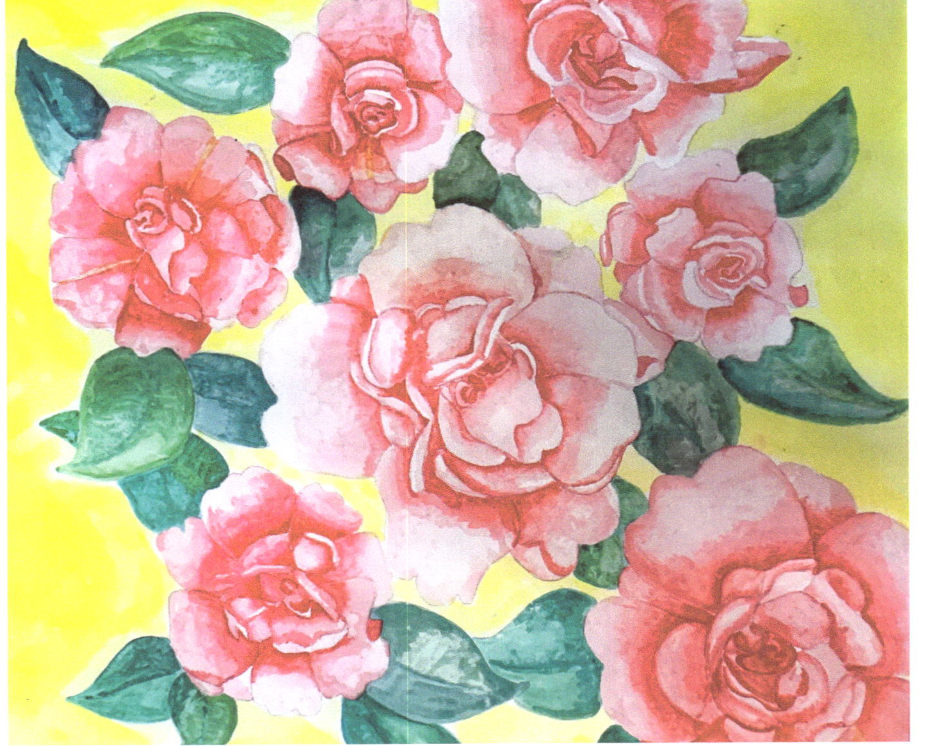

Inpatient Roses

able to focus on pictures of roses as I was painting them. It was as if I were unconsciously distracting myself from my thoughts, so I could take needed time to regulate myself and then come back to the work I needed to do.

I realized Art Therapy also helped me to recognize, investigate, and develop ways to manage behaviors and feelings; to improve self-acceptance; and to help individuals like me to express themselves. There are many areas where Art Therapy can help improve the lives of clients who may be affected by trauma, anxiety, depression, chronic illnesses, or physical or mental health concerns.

Art Therapists are trained in a variety of areas, including Art Therapy theories; human development; psychological theories; therapeutic processes; behavioral, spiritual and multi-cultural traditions; and much more.

The benefits of Art Therapy to its clients are endless. For the purpose of this book, and for me personally, Art Therapy is defined as a form of expression, along with communicating to others working with me in my healing process. Art Therapy helped me explore and grow from a very traumatic experience. When defining Art Therapy, I feel it is very important to explain the process I went through, and the meaning behind each piece of my artwork as it became a very valuable part of my healing. Working on a piece of art along with the Art Therapist, psychologist, and therapist gave me that opportunity to deeply explore the true meanings behind my artwork, and how it opened doors for me. I found that this is the best way for me to express and define what Art Therapy is and how it was used to help me to heal.

In this sketch, *dance of two*, I was trying to express my feelings, and be okay in doing just that, *expressing feelings*. The *dance of two* is really about observing that I really have sadness, shame, fear, and anger. I was being introduced to DBT skills as I was learning to observe and describe my emotions. The more I was learning DBT Skills, I found Art Therapy helped me to solidify the meaning of the skills. I did this by using my art to help me to communicate what I was learning to Neal. Once I understood, Neal took the next steps to educate me in how to use these feelings in a healthy way as I incorporated them into my life—this was the beginning of *feeling the feels*. I truly believe I was never in touch with my feelings—I didn't even know I had them.

I often said I never got angry. As mentioned earlier, Dr. Laura said, the first time she met me, I had no connection to what was happening with my feelings within me, or understanding how to feel the emotions. It was here that I began to connect to my Art Therapy and the use of DBT skills to help me grow.

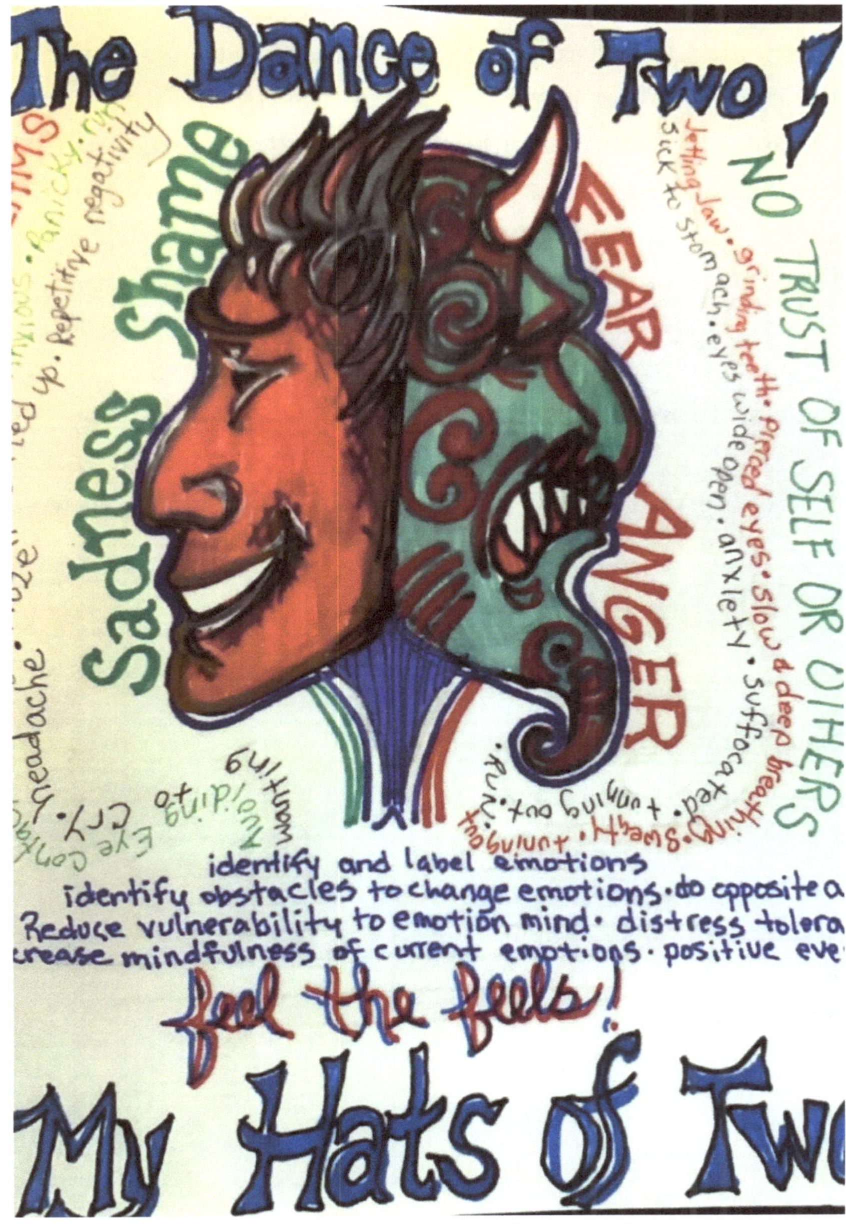

The art work below, *Loss*, has many emotions incorporated in it. To me it shows how Art Therapy and other forms of creative therapies can assist in healing. In this picture of the eye, the feeling of shame is encapsulated by a tear. I connected the words and their meanings by using my doodling with a black ink pen. Art Therapy helped me to express my pain and fear that was so prevalent in my life for so many years. The connection of my pain radiated with the feeling of loss. More importantly, it shows that all along, my art was connecting to my emotions. In therapy, I learned new skills to see how important it was to "rescue the brain" by refeeding. It was the nutrition and rescuing the brain that helped me cognitively understand the relationship of my pain and the connection to my feelings of loss. Later in treatment, I saw, within the same drawing, how I intuitively used positive quotes and sayings that encircled the word "loss." I was able to see this when Neal taught me the importance of another DBT tool called **corrective information**. This tool taught me to observe my negative self-talk, then use corrective information to immediately challenge the negative thought with factual information. This assists in breaking the negative thought patterns. This literally opened my eyes to the value of Art Therapy and how each piece of my drawing connects to myself and how my artwork helped me to express myself. It was then it became apparent that I was getting in touch with my emotions.

Loss

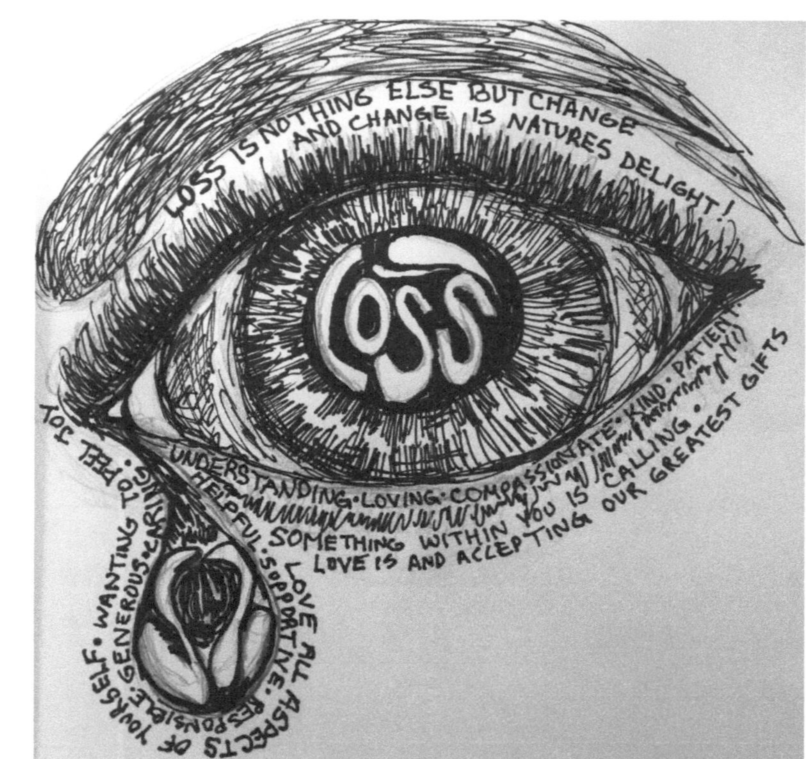

The word I chose in my doodle, "Loss," focused on corrective information. I found some very strong insight to my thoughts and beliefs as I processed my artwork while adding corrective information. This process provided me additional validation to my feelings and the pain I felt. To identify that I felt loss and shame doesn't mean I have to like it, I'm just validating myself, along with radically accepting that I have these emotions. The words around the eye are all about understanding these emotions, while providing compassion for myself. Most of my life I searched for validation from others. I found when I'm dealing with loss and shame, I have to look at validating myself. I learned to radically accept my feelings, then provide the love and compassion that included all the good things about myself—the things that I value and live by on a daily basis—acknowledging that I am lovable and that I have a lot of people supporting me. I was beginning to learn a lot about the feelings I feared. When I am able to validate myself and my feelings, I provide myself opportunities for self-compassion as well. This was a great way to start loving myself—which was long overdue.

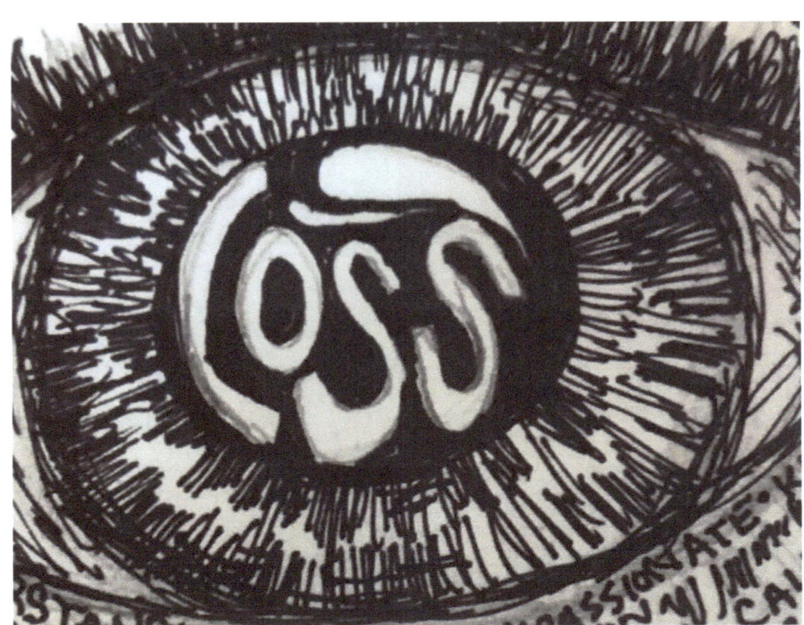

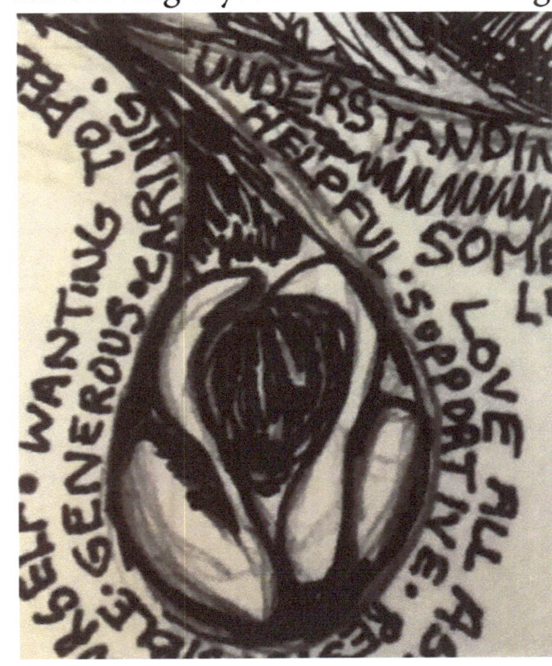

As I continued to look and process my artwork, I first was struggling with the concept of loss— I was unconsciously connecting to how I was feeling. I so much wanted to cry, but my tears were stifled. I was too sick to really understand what my art already could voice. I needed to let go and cry. As I worked with Dr. Laura, we would focus on the eye, as if my eyes were wide open to the shame. I was feeling the loss that came from my illness and trauma. At the time I drew this piece, I was not connected to my feelings. Everything seemed so glassed over. When I utilized the positive words and corrective information, Dr. Laura helped me to explore and identify what I was unable to express verbally. My art found the true feelings of my pain and suffering. It was as if my eyes were wide open to the pain when I drew the eye; I surrounded the pain with positive language as a form of distraction. Now that I am healthier, I am cognitively able to see the connection. I could accept that, as I drew in that very moment, I was feeling the loss and shame. I could not find the words to openly express my feelings. Now, when I see this doodle, I see the positive words written throughout the art piece. I also see that I am now more willing to make the changes needed, to use corrective information. This leads me down the path of growth, self-acceptance, self-love, and healing.

This picture, *popcorn*, is a playful piece, tongue-in-cheek. I spent many therapeutic hours working on my need to always be on the go, and my brain just never stopped. This acrylic painting was an abstract version of popcorn. I connected to the constant need to be on the go as a way to disconnect, being too busy to feel. The popcorn was my rendition of how my brain worked…

popcorn

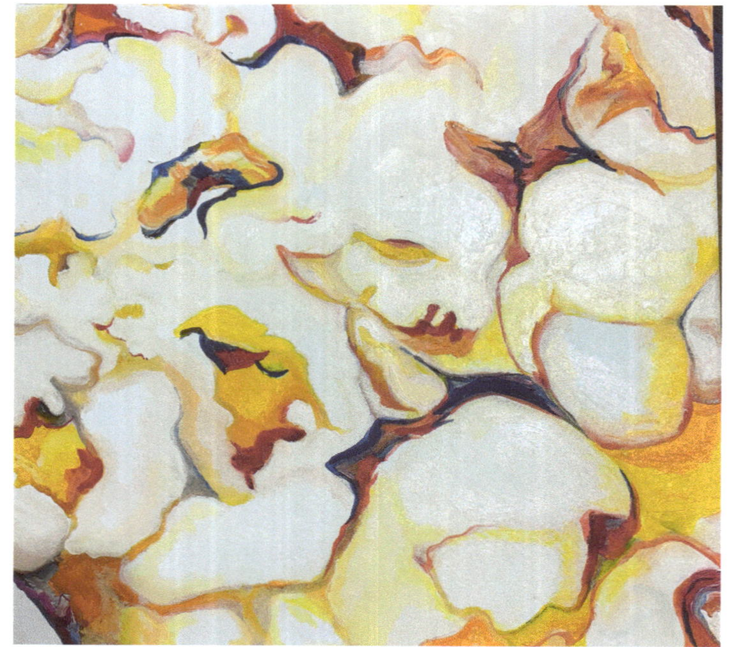

Art Therapy is used in hospitals, mental health facilities, treatment centers, psychotherapy sessions, rehabilitation centers, and much more. Art Therapy has been used with a wide range of clients, including children, adults, the elderly, individuals with disabilities, and mental health and/or behavioral disabilities. The growth of Art Therapy has now found benefits in programs for veterans and trauma victims. Art Therapists are trained in several techniques and approaches, including basic areas of human development, child development, and behavioral and mental health needs.

As part of my education, I became a Registered Art Therapist. I found my passion focused in on one aspect of Art Therapy, which was to provide opportunities for individuals with special needs. I thank my younger brother for this, as I learned many things from him. He grew to be a strong, loving individual through the difficulties of being born deaf. I was always inspired by his ability at such a young age; how he didn't look at challenges as obstacles. He faced the world as if he were unaware of any roadblocks in his life. It was my brother and my parents that tackled those roadblocks. It was their determination to provide him the same opportunities as his hearing peers.

I especially learned from my mother, who was determined to find any and every avenue to make life easier and successful for my brother. I took this lesson early in life, I was determined to make opportunities for each individual I worked with; to work with what they needed, but also with their abilities, so I could provide them the experiences to feel that sense of accomplishment and success.

Art Therapy is a great tool for clients who experience challenges in everyday life due to their individualized needs and abilities. I identify my Art Therapy with clients, to individuals who have physical or developmental disabilities, chronic illnesses, or are on the autism spectrum. While creating art and working toward the process, each client can build on their self-acceptance and learn to cope with their behavior or symptoms and the challenges in their lives. The clients I work with in my Art Therapy practice build cognitive and emotional strength. They enjoy making art while learning from the therapeutic process.

My clients are also my inspiration to strive for a life worth living. They have shown me determination with how they work through their challenges, and I see their successes on a daily basis. Below, you will see some artwork from my clients. Each client has their own style, and I am so proud of them and their work. This is just an example of how amazing Art Therapy is, and no matter what their challenges may be, they can use art as their tool of expression.

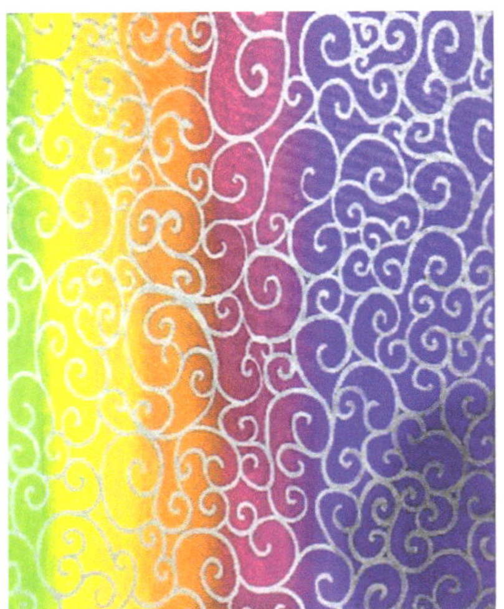
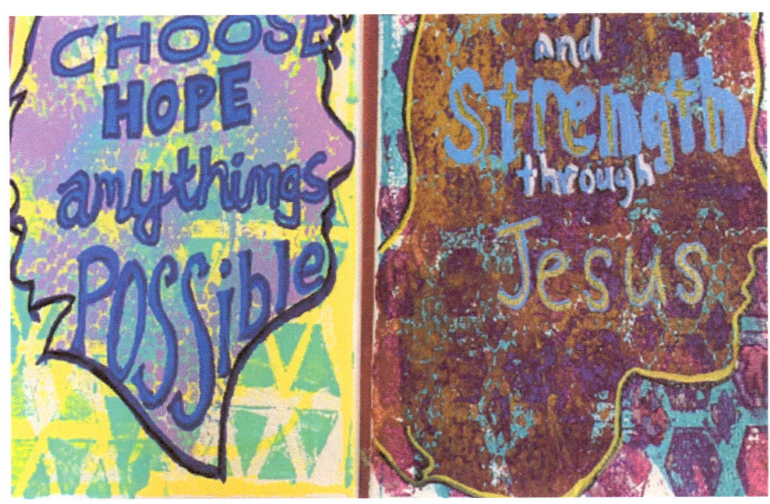

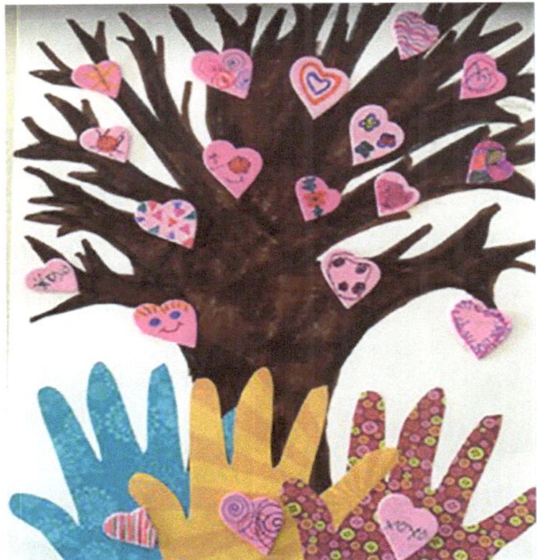

I continue to realize that I am blessed to be an Art Therapist who can reach out to clients with special needs. Just working side-by-side with clients with disabilities, autism, or chronic illnesses, helps me not only to acknowledge but to share in my calling, and that is one of my strongest attributes. It gives me an opportunity to step back from life and my traumatic experiences. Again, this is only one avenue of Art Therapy that is being used.

Another approach to Art Therapy can be demonstrated by my own healing process. Art Therapy brought awareness of my emotions, and it helped me process, metaphorically and/or symbolically, different ways to tell my story. The key was in the process of Art Therapy, along with Dr. Laura, who helped me to see and interpret my drawing/paintings. It was then I could see and benefit from the art as I explored the meanings behind my own art. This process provided what I so longed for, a voice to tell my story.

My discussion of Art Therapy is how I use it in my journey, as well as the specialized area of my profession; it is by no means a complete account of the field of Art Therapy.

The following information is from the American Art Therapy Association:

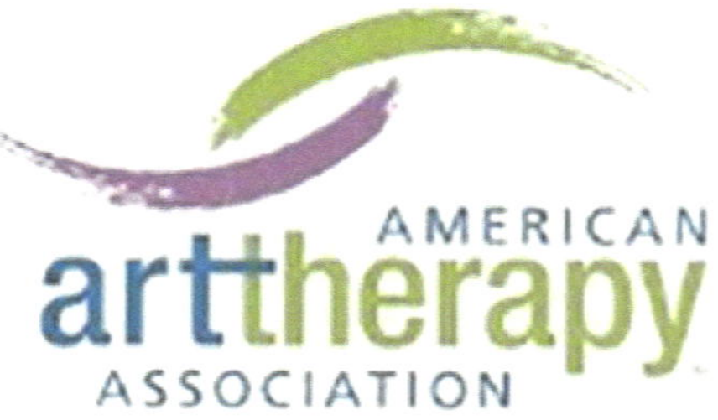

Definition: Organization:

The American Art Therapy Association is a not-for-profit, professional and educational organization dedicated to the growth and development of the Art Therapy profession. Founded in 1969, The American Art Therapy Association is one of the world's leading Art Therapy membership organizations.

(Concise) Definition of Art Therapy:

Art Therapy is an integrative mental health and human services profession that enriches the lives of individuals, families, and communities through active art-making, creative process, applied psychological theory, and human experience within a psychotherapeutic relationship.

Art Therapy, facilitated by a professional art therapist, effectively supports personal and relational treatment goals as well as community concerns. Art Therapy is used to improve cognitive and sensory-motor functions, foster self-esteem and self-awareness, cultivate emotional resilience, promote insight, enhance social skills, reduce and resolve conflicts and distress, and advance societal and ecological change.

(Broader) Definition of Art Therapy:

Art Therapy is an integrative mental health and human services profession that enriches the lives of individuals, families, and communities through active art-making, creative process, applied psychological theory, and human experience within a psychotherapeutic relationship.

Art Therapy, facilitated by a professional art therapist, effectively supports personal and relational treatment goals as well as community concerns. Art Therapy is used to improve cognitive and sensory-motor functions, foster self-esteem and self-awareness, cultivate emotional resilience, promote insight, enhance social skills, reduce and resolve conflicts and distress, and advance societal and ecological change.

Art therapists are master-level clinicians who work with people of all ages across a broad spectrum of practice. Guided by ethical standards and scope of practice, their education and supervised training prepares them for culturally proficient work with diverse populations in a variety of settings. Honoring individuals' values and beliefs, Art Therapists work with people who are challenged with medical and mental health problems, as well as individuals seeking emotional, creative, and spiritual growth.

Through integrative methods, Art Therapy engages the mind, body, and spirit in ways that are distinct from verbal articulation alone. Kinesthetic, sensory, perceptual, and symbolic opportunities invite alternative modes of receptive and expressive communication, which can circumvent the limitations of language. Visual and symbolic expression gives voice to experience, and empowers individual, communal, and societal transformation.

(Updated June, 2017. Source: www.arttherapy.org)

CHAPTER FIVE

DBT and My Part in Kathleen's Journey

by Neal Moglowsky

*Licensed Professional Counselor, Linehan-Certified DBT Clinician,
President of the Center for Behavioral Medicine, Kathleen's DBT Therapist*

<u>What is Dialectical Behavior Therapy?</u>

DBT is a mindfulness-based, cognitive behavioral therapy first published in 1993 by Dr. Marsha Linehan, PhD. DBT was developed to treat chronically suicidal individuals diagnosed with borderline personality disorder (individuals who struggle regulating their emotions, thoughts, behaviors, sense of self, and relationships). It is a comprehensive, multi-module treatment, which involves five different components:

- Emotional Skills Training Group
- Individual Psychotherapy
- Skills Coaching outside of Regularly scheduled therapy sessions
- Consultation Team
- Ancillary Treatments not involving the first four components (i.e., medication management, dietician consultation, support groups)

In the Emotional Skills Training Group, individuals are taught four sets of skills:

- Mindfulness Skills
- Emotion Regulation
- Distress Tolerance
- Interpersonal Effectiveness Skills

What does Dialectical mean in Dialectical Behavior Therapy?

The concept of dialectics refers to life constantly having two polar-opposite perspectives that are both valid and true at the same time. It's the opposite of black and white…and it's not seeing gray…it's more like seeing plaid. The main dialectic in DBT is to balance the need to validate and accept the client for exactly where they are at and that they are doing their best, and at the same time, they need to learn skills and work harder to change the things that need to change.   Life has emotion and logic at the same time. My wife has a perspective that is valid, and I have a perspective that is valid…both at the exact same time. I love my kids, and they drive me insane…both at the exact same time.

The beginning stages and structure of DBT

DBT is a principle-driven treatment, as opposed to a manual-driven treatment. Each individual's treatment is set up for their individual issues and personality. It isn't cookie-cutter. There is a structure, and it is individualized and supported to what the client's exact needs are (that's a dialectic in itself).

Clients begin this treatment after both the client and therapist make a collaborative agreement to, at a minimum, work on solving life's problems in ways that don't involve suicide or self-harming behaviors. After all, if you are dead, nothing else matters, and the treatment won't work. Clients sign an initial one-year contract, at the end of which, we review treatment, evaluating if we are getting where we want to go. The overall arching goal of treatment is for the client to build a life that they experience as worth living. The client does not get more DBT treatment unless there is progress being made towards these life-worth-living goals. If the client is not progressing using DBT, we would refer them to a different type of therapy.

Clients don't fail treatment; the treatment fails the client

In medicine, if a treatment is not working, the doctors don't just keep doing more of it, they change the treatment. DBT is the same way. If the treatment isn't making progress for someone, we evaluate and try to figure out what's getting in the way. Maybe DBT isn't the right treatment for that person. Maybe there is something else going on that is more relevant, like a substance abuse problem and the client needs to be referred to a substance abuse program. Sometimes the therapist isn't conducting therapy to fidelity. In Kathleen's case, her eating disorder was so destructive to her mind and body that she needed to be re-fed; to get enough nutrition so that her brain could work correctly. Kathleen's brain was not functioning well enough initially to fully learn and integrate the DBT skills she was being taught. There are a number of factors that get in the way of people being motivated to do the treatment. Sometimes the environment they are living in may not be supportive. Sometimes loved ones lack skills themselves. DBT believes that if the treatment doesn't work, it is the fault of the treatment.

The primary problem that DBT treats is the inability to regulate emotions which is believed to be a result of a transaction between both biological and social/environmental factors. It is theorized that, as a result of these factors, the client experiences their emotions in a much more intense way. They are more emotionally sensitive in that it takes a smaller cue to evoke an emotion, and when an emotion is set off, it is experienced more reactively …like tapping the gas pedal on a top-fuel dragster…emotions get very intense very fast, and because they are so intense, it takes a longer time to reregulate back to their emotional baseline after an emotion has fired off. As a result, clients develop a number of troublesome belief systems, behavioral patterns, and skills deficits. Without adding new skills to their current coping repertoire they will get stuck in these patterns which lead to tremendous misery and suffering.

The role of skills training group is to teach those skills, typically in a group setting. I often tell my clients that they are signing up for Emotions 101. Clients typically attend skills group weekly for 2-2½ hours per week during which they are learning four main skill sets: core-mindfulness, emotion regulation, distress tolerance, and interpersonal effectiveness. They are taught each skill at least twice.

They also, of course, have an individual therapist whose job it is to take the skills taught in the group, and apply them to the patient's individual life situations. Within the individual treatment, individuals have a "diary card" which tracks all of the target behaviors that client might engage in to seek relief from whatever the distress is that is going on in their life. We begin each session by reviewing the diary card, and whenever a target behavior comes up, we spend time working through what we call "Behavioral Chain Analysis." We take a behavior and walk through what led up to the target behavior so we can really determine what is controlling or driving the person to act on the target behavior. It's getting to the true definition of the problem that needs to be treated.

"The person said this to you. What fired off inside of you next? What were your body sensations? What were your thoughts? Then, what happened next?" It is a chain of events that we put in order. I use the term "emotional Rube Goldberg Machine": this thought sets off this body sensation, sets off this action, sets off this thought, and we get the chain of what happened not only outside, but also internally. As we identify all the links in the chain, we then teach the client how to take the skills they are learning in DBT skills training group and intervene at those "controlling variables."

If we can treat the controlling variables…those key dominoes…the chain stops and the dominos don't fall. The more we can help the individual identify what their links are and what links keep showing up on the chain of events, they get better and better at being able to catch them, observe they are happening, and intervene quicker and quicker.

In addition, clients have the ability to get skills coaching with their individual therapist, outside of scheduled sessions, to get assistance in real-life situations where they are struggling and need some help with applying the skills when needed most. We encourage our clients to call before their struggle becomes a crisis. We are explicitly clear with them that we don't want them to wait for their crisis to become a self- harm or suicidal event. Often, when they call, there has been some sort of specific stressor, such as an argument with a loved one or another difficulty in life. As a result of that situation, combined with their emotional sensitivity, reactivity, and slow return to baseline, combined with a lack of skills, they may become very emotionally dysregulated. When you are dysregulated, you can't think straight and can't problem-solve. Often in these times, clients are more likely to have impulsive urges such as self-harming, drinking, eating disorder behavior, or other urges meant to help them reregulate. The behaviors often serve the same function, it helps them reregulate in some form. When they call, they often say something to the effect of, "I'm 'freaking out!'" and/or "I want to do some impulsive self-destructive behavior!" But they realistically aren't asking for help to do that as much as they are trying to get some help to not do whatever that targeted impulsive behavior is. They often are calling for help to reregulate. Typically, after getting a brief description of the problem, the therapist and client are able to identify what skills to use and how to use them, develop a plan and obtain a commitment to implement that plan. The client is supported in putting it into action, and the client and situation can reregulate. The crisis is averted, the target behaviors don't happen, and more extensive mental health services aren't needed.

The fourth component is Consultation Team, which is DBT Therapy for the therapists. If we are stuck at some point in an individual's therapy, I have the entire team to help me work through that. They help me make sure I am doing DBT to fidelity, to help me get un-stuck, and to make sure that I manage my own emotions, frustrations, and judgements during the therapy. My team is there to make sure that I am staying behaviorally compassionate and validating.

The fifth component involves anything not included in the first four. This may include ancillary treatments, such as medication management, support groups, or dietitians. DBT is not a medical model, and a psychiatrist is not the head of the treatment team. That role belongs to the individual therapist. In Kathleen's case, ancillary treatments include medication management, a specific Eating Disorders Therapist, and a dietician.

DBT research and adaptations

Over time, DBT has gone through an extensive amount of research. Repeated randomized controlled trials show this is a treatment that helps people refrain from engaging in a number of impulsive behaviors, including suicidal behaviors; it decreases the need for in-patient hospitalizations and other higher levels of care. There have been adaptations for eating disorders, adolescents, children, substance use, and older adults; there is a DBT protocol to teach DBT as an additional health class in middle schools; there is an adolescent program that has the kids and parents learn the DBT skills together. In short, DBT is an empirically based treatment with a tremendous amount of research to back up its effectiveness. It is important to note however that Marsha Linehan, the treatment developer, would say, "DBT is not an anti-suicide program, it's a life-worth-living program!" It is not enough to just be alive. We have to solve the problems that are causing the misery and suffering.

Kathleen's response to DBT

Specifically, Kathleen has made spectacular progress with her DBT. One of the great areas of growth that Kathleen is identifying is that she has a number of escape and avoidance behaviors that she uses to stop feeling the intense emotional distress that she lives in. One of her most powerful insights is that her treatment isn't about not purging or not self-harming, it is much more about needing to start feeling. She has made great gains, especially since we began working on her trauma, which in the past she simply was not able to do because she couldn't tolerate the emotion. As she has gotten better and better at the skills, she is able to start to process through some of the traumas in her past. She is now able to feel the emotions that she could never feel before. She's teaching her mind more and more: I can do this, I can accept this, I can't tolerate this, and the emotions aren't going to destroy me. That has enabled her to go to other places as far as accepting herself and getting out from under all of the self-blame that she often gets herself stuck in. It is hard for a client to correct information and change beliefs when there are certain places that one can't go. As Kathleen has gotten some of her behaviors under control, we've been able to go to some of these other places she hasn't been able to previously.

The initial stage of DBT focuses on trying to get behaviors under control; to extinguish the self-harming behaviors. Kathleen's purging behavior has nearly killed her multiple times. We had to get these under control first; I can't do trauma work with someone who is either dead or in a coma, and Kathleen has been in a coma several times as a result of aspiration pneumonia from her purging.

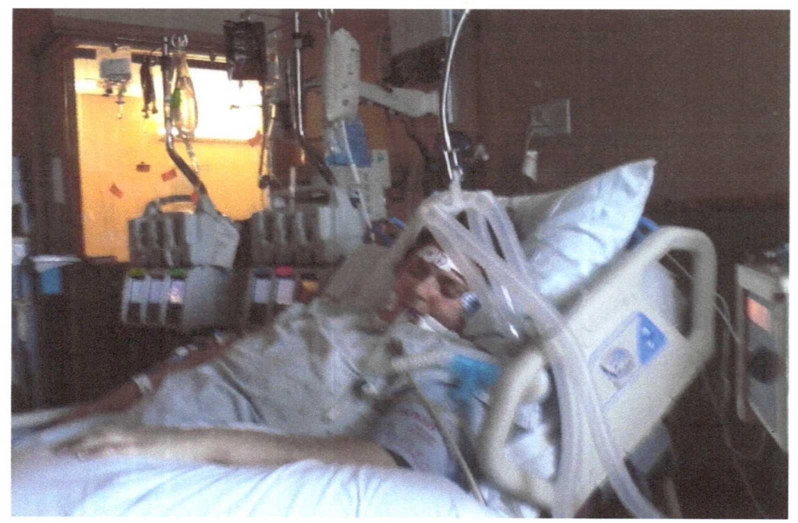

We also needed to address Kathleen's dissociative behavior; Dissociation is a behavior which happens when the mind shuts down from an emotion that is so intense that it just can't tolerate it. So, our initial steps of treatment focused on getting skills on board so she could begin to tolerate the emotions of everyday living before we could start to do trauma work. You can't open up Pandora's Box unless the person has the skills to deal with what comes out. If the person is not ready, then that person will be re-traumatized.

Kathleen has made spectacular progress in terms of not engaging in self-harming behavior. We still have some work to do on some of her eating disorders and dissociating, but these behaviors are much more infrequent and not near the severity of what they were in the past.

While the initial stage of DBT is about getting the impulsive behaviors under control, stage two—where Kathleen is currently—is much more about starting to experience and process emotions and trauma. As we entered this stage of treatment, some of her self-harming behaviors reappeared as we started to do more trauma work exposing her to her fears and flashbacks. We've been able to navigate through those struggles, and she is now able to discuss intimate details of the most painful moments of her life. She is able to do this with feeling, which she could never do before.

The metaphor Marsha Linehan uses, at times, to describe clients is as if they are "emotional burn victims." The slightest touch causes excruciating pain for them. Kathleen and I will often talk about the goal of her treatment is not to feel better, but to get her better at feeling. She has gotten better and better at feeling. That is the bulk of what we're working on.

Kathleen is experiencing more than she ever has, and we are able to process events that she falsely blamed herself for. Now she is able to put what happened to her in a greater level of context, to share more and reveal more and correct her faulty beliefs about herself which have led to so much pain and suffering for years. Even the writing of this book is a huge sign of how far she has come.

Our therapeutic relationship and radical genuineness

In DBT, there is a concept called "Radical Genuineness." One of the aspects of this is to respect our clients enough that they can handle the truth. We don't help our clients by distorting reality or somehow setting up their world so it is not actually based in reality. There are times when Kathleen says something that is B.S., or ridiculous in some way, but we have a secure enough relationship where I can say, "Now c'mon, Kathleen, that's bulls#!t." She even bought me a B.S. button that I will hit from time to time. When I hit it, Kathleen immediately knows, in a playful way, that she is missing the mark, has fallen into an old pattern, or is invalidating herself, and can then immediately correct that distorted thought or ineffective action. I am treating her like she is a capable and competent person, who can handle the truth and handle reality because she needs to handle the truth and reality. I want to teach her how to deal with life on life's terms, whether it involves everyday struggles or triggers of her past trauma.

Using irreverence is always, first and foremost, built on a bedrock of validation and acceptance and compassion. I think that is something that Kathleen and I grew into, although, neither of us are really sure of the exact origin. It is just a process that is established over time. I know Kathleen had a different type of relationship with the therapist she saw before me. We have different styles, and Kathleen was angry when we first started working together because I told her we weren't going to talk, we were going to get to work. She had a tough time with that at first, but then she realized she was learning and that was exciting to her. She was hungry to learn more. She found my style worked for her.

The therapeutic relationship in DBT is meant to be a real relationship. I do get on her case, but I think that speaks to the relationship that we have. For many clients, a main therapeutic task is learning how to have a decent quality, balanced relationship. With Kathleen and me, we step on each other's toes from time to time; we get frustrated with each other; I push her too hard on something, and she makes my head want to explode; and we're also very good at repairing the relationship. The reality is that you can't have an intimate relationship without there being some conflict from time to time and hurt feelings. The goal is not to make sure the person is never upset with you, it's really about accepting that it will happen and, when it does, being committed enough in our relationship that we can talk about it, repair it, and also understand that, at the end of the day, it is all coming from a place of care, concern, and love.

<u>Failing to observe and describe limits: A major quality-of-life-interfering behavior</u>

Another skills deficit that Kathleen has struggled with for most of her life is observing and describing her limits. Her life experiences have taught her that her needs are always secondary, and if she isn't putting others first, it means that she is failing and being a bad person. As a result, Kathleen's greatest asset is her greatest downfall. She is an incredibly caring, compassionate person, and at times she can get taken advantage of. She believes she has a tremendous sense of responsibility for saving the entire world and fixing others' problems. She puts everything for herself and others on her shoulders until she gets overwhelmed, dysregulated, and burnt out. This has been a pattern that has started so many of the chains that led to target behaviors. We have talked extensively about three behaviors to practice along these lines: stop raising your hand, say no, and delegate and ask others for help. These are patterns that she has started to work on in her friendships and relationships with family as well as with some of the parents of the clients she works with. These things are very difficult for her, and yet, she is now, more than ever, beginning to accurately express her true emotions, to ask for her heartfelt wants and desires, and to say no to requests that realistically she can't fulfill without sacrificing so much of herself that it would actually be harmful.

<u>Kathleen doesn't need to change or get better as much as she is already there</u>

Kathleen and I have often spoken about that DBT isn't about fundamentally changing her. In fact, DBT starts with the perspective that she is already just fine and is already the person she needs to be. In short…there is nothing wrong with her heart and soul. There is nothing wrong with Kathleen's morals, her values, or her ethics. Through DBT one of the most fundamental discoveries that she is making is that now, more than ever, she is the loving and caring wife she has always been, the dedicated mom who is always there for her kids, the compassionate Art Therapist who fights for and advocates for the needs of her clients, and most importantly, the strong, courageous woman that she has always been. Thank you, Kathleen, for making me not only a better therapist, but a better husband, a better dad, a better friend, and a better man.

The Importance of Art Therapy and DBT Therapy and Finding the Right Therapists

To tie this all together for the purpose of this book, it was here when I also started to bring in my artwork. I'm fortunate to have been blessed with some art skills, and I was able to draw and paint what I was learning. When I started to include my art, it helped me to break down the steps visually, which also helped to determine what I was grasping in sessions. This was not typical for DBT, yet both Neal and Dr. Laura realized how important my artwork was to me and how my processing the art assisted in better communication. This was a "wow moment" for me as I quickly saw that my art helped me to articulate what I was learning, and in some cases, what I wasn't able to say.

Every so often, I brought along my artwork to my sessions, to help communicate back to Neal on what I understood and how I was using the DBT skills that I was learning. It is important to note that Art Therapy was not written into Marsha Linehan's workbook; this just happened to be a very vital tool in my learning what was being taught to me. Then again, Neal did mention earlier, this wasn't a cookie cutter therapy program, and here is where my true journey began.

This chapter tells you a little bit of how I ended up utilizing both Art Therapy and DBT therapy as the tools that I found extremely helpful to make life-changing goals for myself. Initially I thought I would need to find a specific style of therapy. I knew I needed a therapeutic technique or strategy that was a natural fit for me. As an educator and a Registered Art Therapist I needed not only the technique to fit my visual learning style, but also a therapist whose style would motivate me to learn. I had one therapist before Neal. She was kind, nurturing, more of a mother figure, and I loved her dearly. When she retired, I was transitioned to her partner Neal. This was definitely my wake-up call. One of Neal's very first comments he made to me was, "We don't come here to just talk, we come here to work." At this time in my life, I was not much for cursing, yet at that moment I was certainly thinking about starting. (As a matter of fact, I think it was a year later that I spent a whole session knocking out swear words with Neal, which was to help me get to the level of intensity I needed to express how I was feeling in some life experiences—now that I was connecting to these feelings.)

Don't get me wrong, it was still a bumpy road in the beginning. When Neal was talking to me, he would quickly pullout his dry erase board to help me to understand many of the DBT concepts and skills. For me, Neal's style to use visual learning was perhaps the key to my first steps of understanding DBT. He was very quick to pull out that dry erase board where he could challenge some of my thoughts by mapping out what I said and organizing it back into DBT terms. Having Neal incorporating the dry erase board as part of his approach to therapy was the connection I needed. Sometimes I would take pictures with my phone of his whiteboard so I could study it more later. Having a therapist who used visual learning was key for me. As a visual learner I preferred having images, pictures with different colors, maps; all sorts of different ways to organize the information he was providing me. This helped in breaking it down to the style of how I processed information. Thinking back to it, it was like he was using his own form of Art Therapy to teach me DBT. It might've not been pictures, but it was his sharing in the visual manner that grabbed my attention. This was valuable to me because I'm very visual. As a matter of fact, I remember one of the first times after starting to work with Neal that everything was coming together—Neal and his whiteboard, along with his style of laying out the steps for me to understand.

Let me give you an example of the first time everything fell in place, and it might've been the most simplistic piece of art I've done, but it was a wow moment for me as it was my way of saying, *I get it*. My artwork was saying, *I grasp the concept of what you're trying to teach me*, and that was exciting. So, at this particular time, we were working on the STOP skill of DBT, which falls under the area of distress tolerance. It was important for me to use this skill as it helped me observe and notice what emotions I was having that triggered or pushed me to wanting to use an ineffective behavior or to become impulsive. The STOP skill stands for: **S**TOP, **T**ake a step back, **O**bserve, and **P**roceed mindfully. Many times, I responded to life in a go-go-go style, never slowing down enough to see what probably was right in front of me. If you don't slow down, you don't get the opportunity to observe what is triggering you. So it was maybe a simplistic way of looking at things, but very helpful to remember this acronym and to really STOP—stop in my tracks so I could begin to see some of my triggers.

To break it down a little bit more, the skill is literally to **STOP and breathe**…the second step of this is to **take a step back** and look at the situation. This was where I often would struggle, since I tend to be an impulsive person, and many times, without thinking, I was in my go-go-go style of function. As I reacted impulsively, I was creating a bigger problem in itself. So, by stepping back, it gave me a moment to use my wise mind—the place where reasonable mind and emotion mind overlap. It is the integration of emotion mind and reasonable mind which helps me to assess the situation more clearly.

The next step is to **observe.** You need to take the time to observe your thoughts and feelings without being judgmental of what you were thinking. Just look at the facts surrounding the situation.

The final step is to **proceed mindfully**. I can take the information that I observed, and again, use my wise mind, which helps me connect everything that is going on. By using the STOP skill, we can be in control of our emotions and not react impulsively.

When Neal and I broke down each step, I realized I was learning one of the first skills of DBT. I tended to get excited as things fell in place as I understood the concept more,and how to incorporate it into my life. I wanted to add my spin to the lesson so more individuals could visually see the concept of STOP. Creating something was my way to show Neal that one of my first lessons that he was teaching me had actually sunk in. I don't do anything small! I had my husband literally trace a stop sign so it was the actual size of a stop sign and he cut it out of a thin wood board. I painted the stop sign and then created the symbol that was used in the DBT's workbook in life-size proportion. I was excited to share my artwork. It was designed as a visual to be shared with other clients. One day I came into Neal's office before my session with my STOP sign in a very large garbage bag tied with a bow. I placed it on his desk chair,

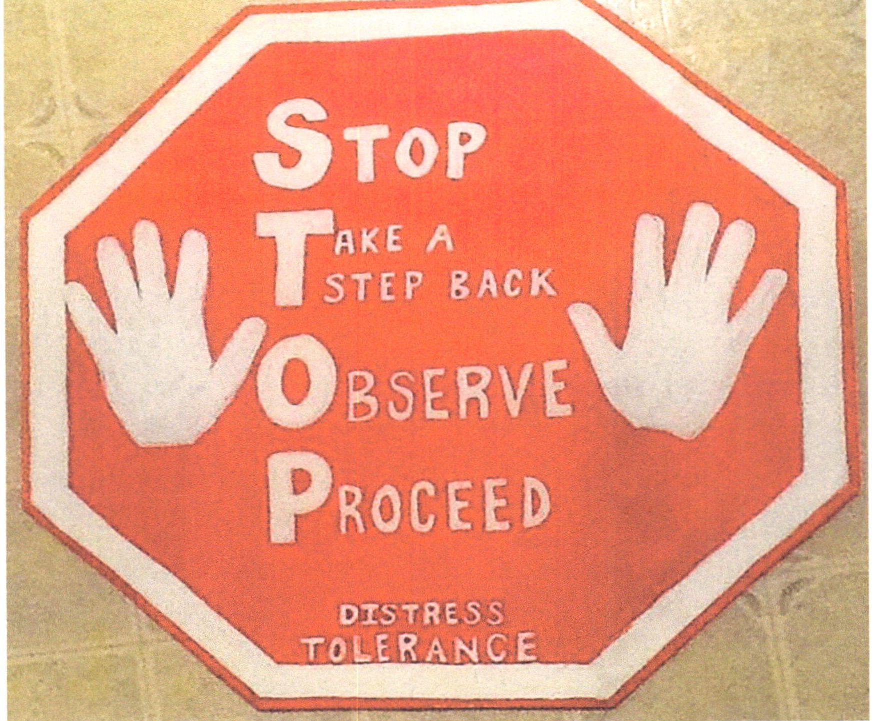

and when he came in for our session, he said, "What's this?" He opened it up, and I don't think I ever heard him laugh so hard. He ran out of the office to show other members of his staff. I think just that alone was giving me the validation that I needed that I truly was getting what he was teaching. Something as simple as painting a stop sign that incorporated the meaning of the skill, was my first step to using my Art Therapy to help solidify the concept of one of DBT's basic skills, and to acknowledge that I understood the skill.

I quickly learned how important it was to find a particular technique of therapy that fit my style to help me to learn and to take that information and incorporate it into my life and experiences that I had. Just as important is the style or technique being used by the therapist. This piece gave me insight that I needed to understand the connection of Art Therapy and DBT therapy and how the two could work together. It was not long before I realized I was learning new skills from Neal, and many times I could reiterate what I was learning to Dr. Laura through my art.

Dr. Laura was also good at connecting the DBT skills I was learning to my art and she helped me process the feelings expressed in my art to my eating disorder behaviors, and how the skills I was learning helped me to challenge my eating disorder-thinking, which I had lived with for way too many years.

Having my therapist work with me on the DBT skills opened many doors for me; but what incorporated the lesson into my everyday life, was to put it into a sketch, a painting, or in some other form of creative expression that expressed my growth and knowledge of what Neal was teaching me.

I realized Art Therapy and my therapists, Neal and Dr. Laura, helped me to find a sense of direction, and to walk the journey I so needed. Utilizing my painting skills also helped me thru some of the hardest work in therapy I have ever done. I continued to create art while Neal began to walk me through and prepare me for another phase of my journey. Neal helped me with Prolonged Exposure (PE) therapy. PE helped me face my trauma-related memories and feelings, and the reality of the experience I endured. For so long, I was living a life of fear. Having Neal take me face to face with the trauma that I went thru, and having me physically be at the location where the trauma happened was beyond comprehension. For a person with PTSD, these memories could trigger flashbacks, panic attacks, and much more when not addressed. The key to prolonged exposure was to teach my mind that the trauma or person could not harm me anymore. The biggest thing I was learning was a new dialogue that played in my head instead of the fears that were ingrained in my memory for so long. I'm thankful I had the opportunity to use PE in my journey. I think PE could be another book for someone to write to tell all of the details of how it works. For me, prolonged exposure was really hard. It challenged me and dared me to take the risk and venture back to the time and experience that changed my life in the direction it was taking. This experience took all the strength I had in me, both in the trust of my therapist, Neal, and to actually having the willingness to walk this journey. It took time and a lot of work to build the trust with Neal that I so needed to take this journey. I am sure it wasn't easy for either of us. Working that hard, I found we built a bond that stood with strength as we entered areas I tried so hard to bury, that I buried so deep that I would dissociate at the thought or triggers of any of its memories. I found this trust helped me to step out of the box a little bit more each time we met. My trauma was my secret that nearly destroyed my life. Yes, I had my eating disorder for the majority of my life; it was my coping mechanism that showed itself any time stress, fear, or loss entered my life. It was because of my experience with trauma that my eating disorder—which I believed protected me—almost destroyed me. The eating disorder tried to cope with my experience; yet, what I thought helped me to control everything, instead took me out of control and I spiraled deep into a black hole. I worked so hard to hide the truth, to keep my professional persona, and to keep the appearance that I had my "stuff" together.

The DBT skills were constantly challenging me, while my art was processing what I needed to learn. The art also taught me to break down the DBT skills and relate how I was growing from the devastating experiences to acceptance and compassion for myself through my art. This was the beauty of the two modalities. DBT not only challenged my thoughts and beliefs, but constantly educated me to re-look at how and why I created these beliefs of mine in the first place. As I implemented my Art Therapy, I felt the visual component helped me to learn and dissect each DBT skill. It was obvious that I was able to learn more from using art as another way to visualize and then comprehend the DBT skills. This combination using both art and DBT methods together helped me to express my own understanding of how to incorporate the skills into my everyday life. It was a beautiful combination.

Through a variety of therapeutic modalities and the art process, Art Therapy engages the mind, body, and spirit in ways that are distinct from verbal articulation alone. I found that Art Therapy provided me the tools to express myself, as it was very difficult to put my emotions and feelings into words. This leads us into my journey that provided the connection of Art Therapy and DBT therapy. Chapter Seven breaks down some of the skills that DBT provided. Skills that I missed in my development both cognitively and emotionally. The process of Art Therapy broke down the skills as I connected to the meaning and the purpose of each DBT skill.

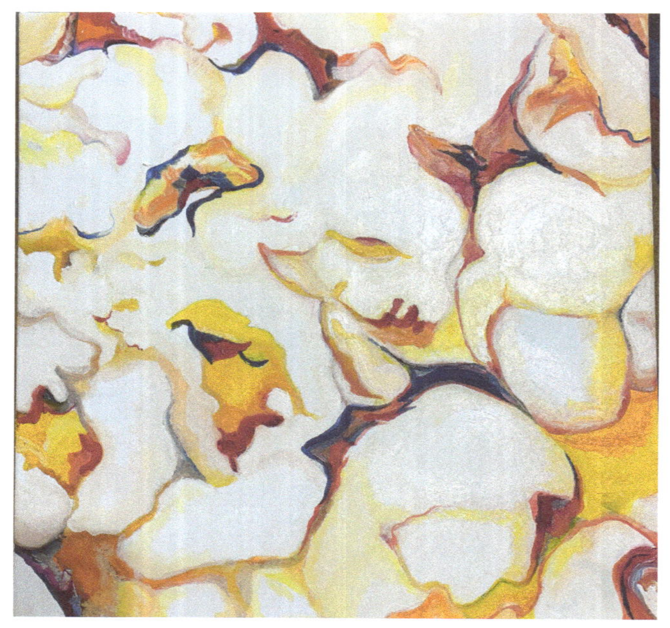

I put this abstract painting in this chapter as an example of how my go-go-go gave me additional compliments from others as I often heard, "How do you do it? You inspire me, because nothing slows you down!" These were not actually ways of complimenting me. These comments added to the myth, that I had it all together. I actually was out of control. It was a myth that my go-go-go made me successful; in actuality it was me running from reality. Yes, deep inside I frantically accomplished a lot, but at what expense—my health!? I loved how this painting demonstrates my mind. I called it *popcorn* because my brain constantly fired off ideas, thoughts, and the list of all the things I had to do. Neal would say I was stuck in a cycle of, "I had to keep busy or else something catastrophic was going to happen." I had days where I tried taking out a few things to slow me down, and then would turn around and fill that space with something else. I was constantly on the go-go-go. I thought it was what made me successful in life. Now I realize the success was the success of being unskillful and not healthy. So my abstract painting was telling me to stop, take a step back, breathe, and observe what I was doing, and proceed mindfully. This is a very difficult thing for me to do. I do work hard at slowing myself down. It is so important to do that and be mindful of what I am doing. It's a myth that the go-go-go was me being productive and successful. What I learned was to stop and be mindful and be the best I could be at what I was doing at the moment. That's more successful.

FINDING MY VOICE

When I found my voice, I found my words which helped me begin to open up and discuss my experience. I thought my eating disorder would protect me but it was destroying me as I was trying to protect those around me from the reality of what I was going through. Initially I found that it was extremely hard to work on my trauma and work on the memories and how that affected me and my loved ones. Secondly, I was sharing the deepest darkest experiences that robbed me, my husband, and my children of the sense of safety associated with this experience. This experience was very intense, and here is where I had to work very hard to find my words, and to learn I was safe; my family was safe. I worked through all these memories with the help of my therapist—a male therapist—that also added another dimension of trust in building a safe environment for processing my memories.

DBT, for me, was about learning how to express myself and learn to feel and acknowledge my feelings that I had kept so buried. My art piece called *Silenced* was also demonstrating how I was learning DBT skills and processing them through my artwork, especially when I felt trapped, voiceless, or needed to scream out.

Silenced

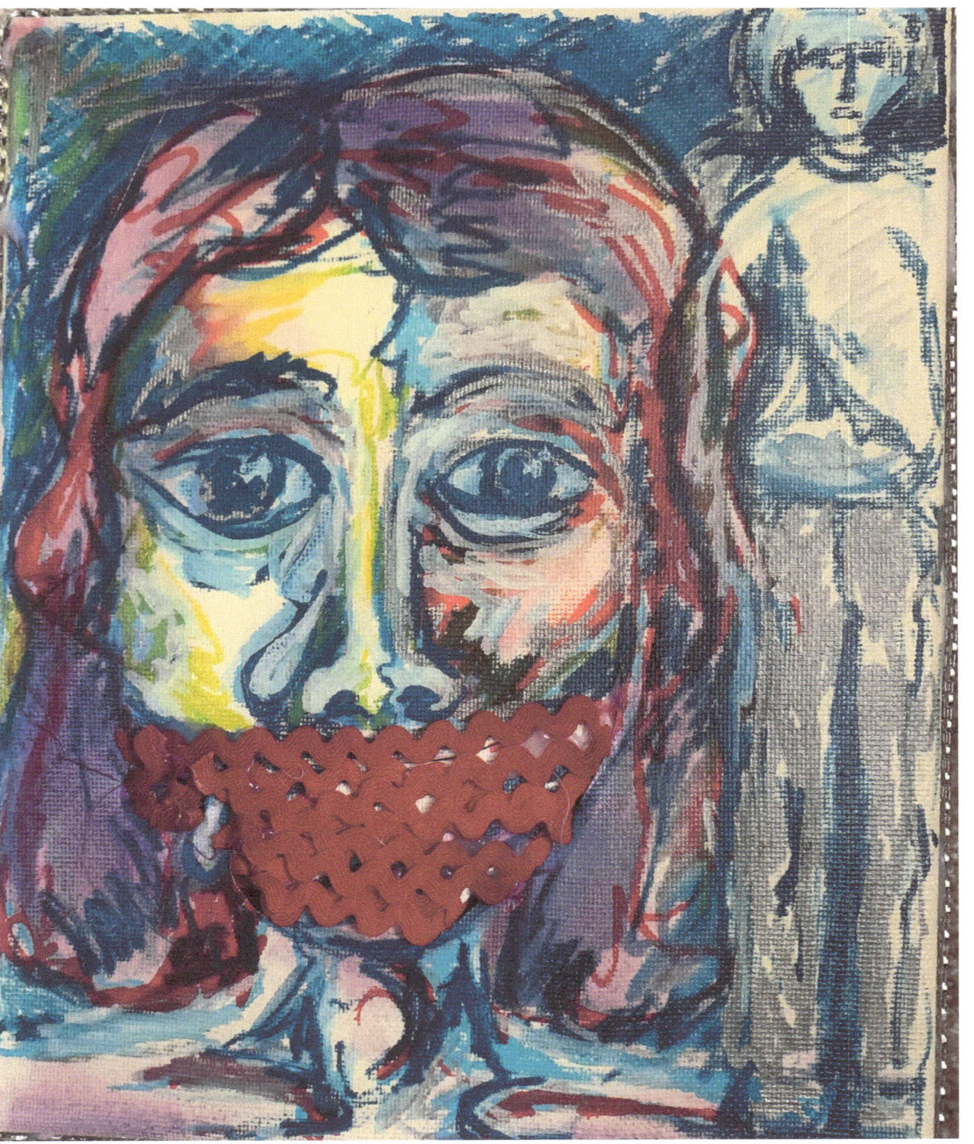

When I break down the steps, I am also learning how to incorporate the DBT skills into my life. I needed to comprehend and learn these skills in order to reach the real goals of having a life worth living. This means getting in touch with my feelings and knowing how each DBT skill is used to help me learn to tolerate distress, while being mindful of my choices.

So, Art Therapy was a natural fit from the beginning, and together, Art Therapy and DBT were the key for me to having a new "check and balance" in a way of learning. The check and balance would let me express what I was learning and how to incorporate the particular DBT skill into dealing with highly emotional situations.

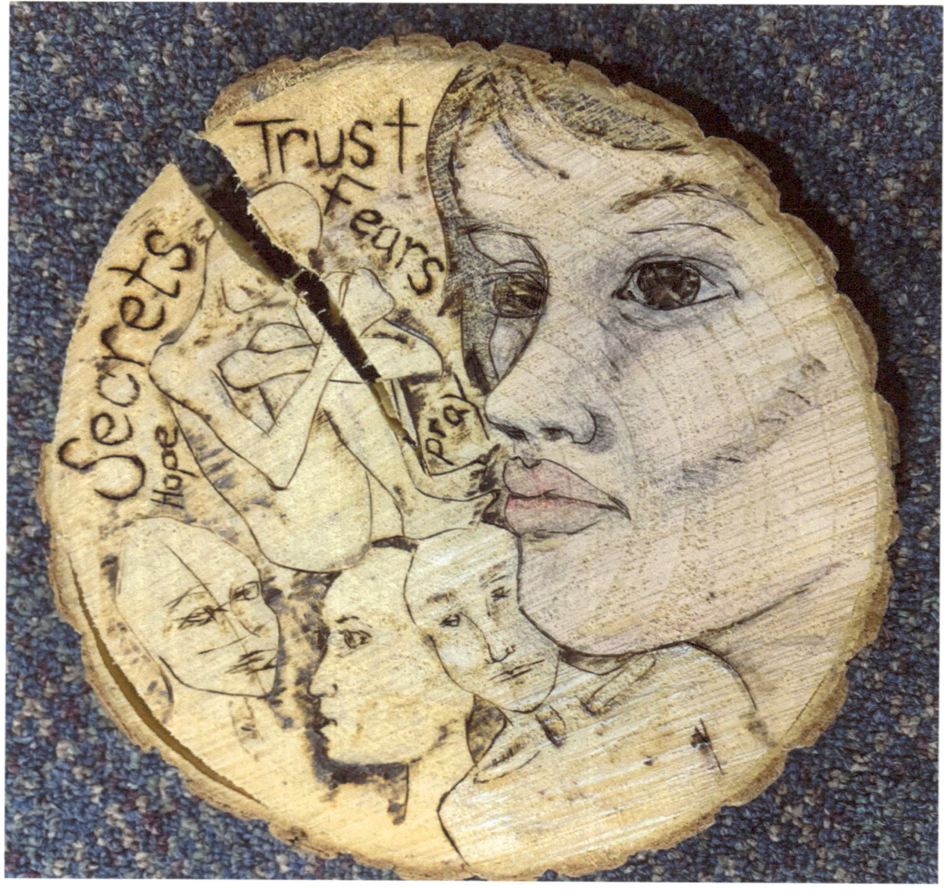

This wood burning was one of my pieces of artwork done while in the hospital for my eating disorder. During that hospital stay, the staff provided the patients' group Art Therapy. Often times it was more open studio, allowing the patients opportunities to express themselves more freely with their own choice of medium. One particular day, I chose to do a wood burning. As I picked out a slab of wood, I happened to come across one that had a split halfway through it. I felt that was exactly how I was feeling: filled with my secrets, too scared to tell what all happened. Fears kept the secrets held within; my pain and suffering were my belief that I needed to protect my loved ones by keeping it secret. I could not trust anyone, I could only pray that my silent scream would somehow be figured out by someone who could voice my secrets. My own pain was the secrets I kept. I had nowhere to go, and at the time, no one to trust. I wanted to scream the words, but nothing came out. I feared I was losing the battle, I was deep in this dark hole, and needing help.

My therapy with Neal helped with bringing everything together, and as time went on, the challenges became bigger, and the topics I talked about in sessions were pretty intense. I never thought that with the help of Neal and Dr. Laura I would have this amount of insight on how and why I responded to triggers or events the way I did.

Neal helped me to reach so many goals in therapy, it was as if he were like my coach as well. Actually, many times he would use baseball terminology as metaphors during a session. Neal has endless energy, I never knew when he would jump from his chair, for example, and get into a batting stance. This stance was to demonstrate and compare the mechanics of batting to the lesson being taught—as I said, he was very visual. Soon I began seeing how every aspect, every experience that I had in life created the beliefs, thoughts, even the fears I lived by.

It was soon after my epiphany that I solved the world's mystery by combining Art Therapy and DBT, and I felt empowered. So maybe it is not the world's mystery, but it was coming together for me and my journey. It was for the first time, having conversations with Dr. Laura and Neal in therapy sessions, that I felt like a participant in my own treatment—a team player. I can't tell you how exciting that can be, when you reach this point. I realized how much I depended on both Neal and Dr. Laura as they taught me so much. With their help I could stand up to some very scary experiences and unravel so many pieces of the puzzle. I needed the help and insights, plus the expertise of my therapists, so that I could grow with and develop a trusting relationship with them.

Coach

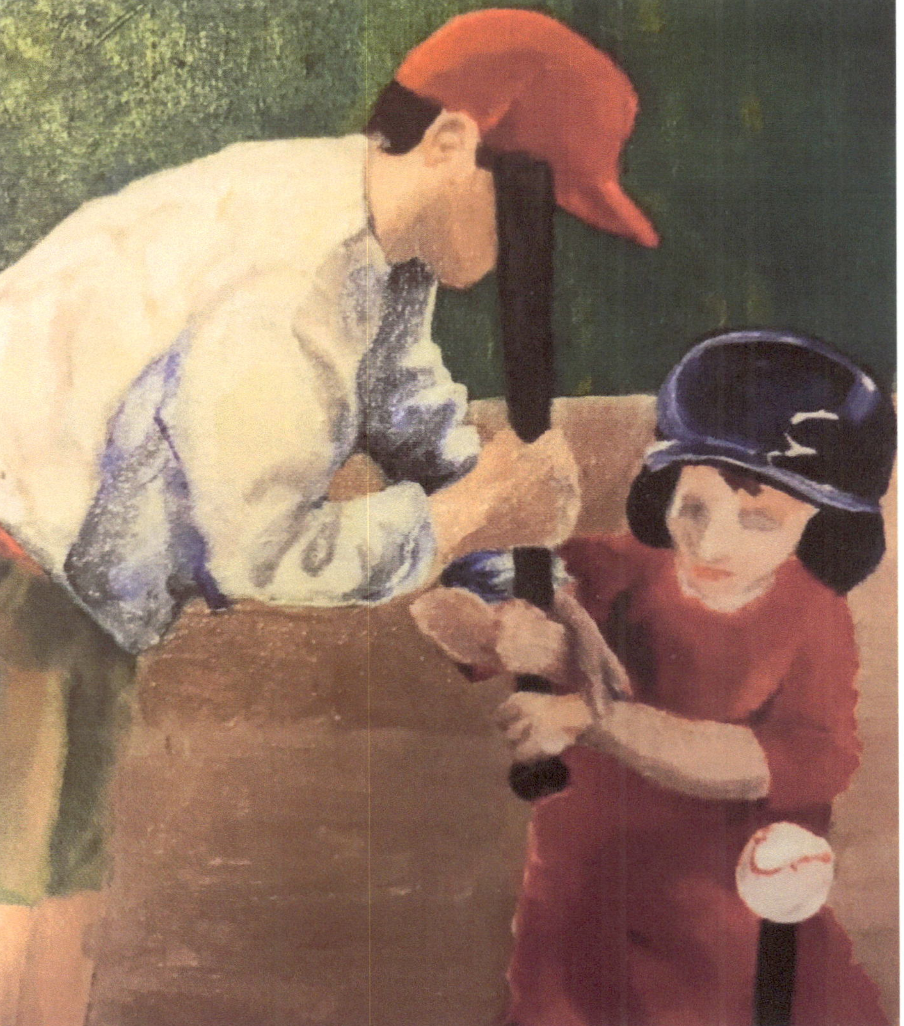

At this level of treatment, both Neal and Dr. Laura quickly began challenging my thoughts, beliefs. Dr. Laura focused on my eating disorder, and Neal focused on many of my life experiences, especially my trauma. Both of them helped me look at how to change my behaviors that were forever ingrained into my reactions and impulses.

I was so excited to come to therapy. I was learning so much, but I still had a lot of fear of rejection as I was sharing my experience, especially opening up to a male therapist, since I felt everything was so private and there was a need to protect myself. The thought of sharing my eating disorder and trauma with someone scared me, as if it would affect my love of work, my passion in helping clients with disabilities. Most of all, letting someone in and trusting them to know the secrets of my behaviors just scared me. I thought every session I was going to get kicked out because I said something wrong…but I kept coming back. I also feared, if I continued to share things, people would know, know all my fears. So, when I say it was a bumpy start—it was because I was scared of everything. Both Neal and I were challenging each other, or maybe it was Neal challenging me, and I was making things challenging by pushing the wrong buttons. Seriously, as we looked into and began challenging my thoughts and getting me to see reality of situations, for me to learn DBT skills was exciting. I challenged Neal with the task of being trustworthy; this is very scary for a client. As clients, we knew that our behaviors were probably ineffective, but for me, they were a way of life. I would be in a session as Neal asked questions or was teaching a DBT skill, and I would ask myself, *if I share this, would I be rejected?* I didn't want to give up. I felt he was my safety net. This was my challenge to Neal. Would I ever be able to trust him? I had a very insecure thought process, and often I would hear only part of what was being said because I would be stuck on one word that distorted the whole conversation. What a whirlwind!

It was like finding another check and balance. As I worked with Neal, he developed exposures which were a form of a lesson that would train my mind to see the facts and that I was safe. This was the hardest work I've ever done in therapy. Therapy became a whole new world for me because I was finding who I was, what I went through, and the skills I needed to develop into a strong woman. Having Neal as my therapist to educate me and take the walk with me through the experiences of my life was huge, and I will forever be thankful to him.

It is just the same having Dr. Laura helping me. She dissected what my eating disorder had done to my health and well-being, and the beliefs and lies that I created as I lived my life through the eyes of my eating disorder. Neal brought me many skills, and he would reach out to Dr. Laura for her insight and her expertise in eating disorders, and that was so important. I could see the whole picture on how not only were Art Therapy and DBT techniques so valuable, but so was finding the right therapists who are willing to walk the walk with me, and not just talk.

I was really enjoying everything Neal was teaching me. To understand DBT skills that were helping me through each step of learning was so invaluable to me. As a visual learner, I found that if I did a piece of artwork expressing the day's lesson and then gave it back to Neal or Laura or both, I was getting validation that I understood what was being taught. Doing this was especially important to working through certain behaviors; it was important to know and have access to Art Therapy that was so soothing and mindful. The visual art put me in a mindset where I could break down when and what I learned in a comprehensive overview of the day's lesson. My artwork is very expressive and gave me a voice to what early on I could not put in words. The combination of Neal's lesson, and my synthesizing the lesson in the form of visual art, gave me a sense of what I learned or did not understand. It was an opportunity to have a discussion through my own artwork to see that I had a better grip of what he was teaching. It soon became my avenue of incorporating the skills into my everyday living. My art confirmed my understanding of the lessons that were being taught to me. It energized me more than you could have imagined. I was motivated to do more learning; I wanted to connect the two styles together. Many times I would hear Neal and Laura saying that I was growing so much and learning so much. They both saw that I had passion for both learning and art; connecting the two was tremendously energizing to me.

It definitely was the beauty of the two: Art Therapy and Dialectical Behavior Therapy. When they came together it was meant to be woven together as a lesson plan just for me. I never did so much art before all of this began.

I felt I had all the powers possible at my fingertips. Neal was teaching me all the skills of core mindfulness, interpersonal effectiveness, emotional regulation, and distress tolerance in a format that was nonjudgmental. Using my skill of the visual art gave me an outlet that was expressive. It didn't challenge how I tried to articulate things, and it didn't challenge my inability to use words; instead it was just the opposite—**it helped me grow in using words!!!!**

Initially, I was intimidated to use certain words, for I had learned it was wrong to say them. As I was growing up, I had the impression that some words were considered wrong, or dirty. What I am trying to say is that when I was given the okay to swear, or use a word that might be too descriptive, it was allowing me to start expressing myself to the intensity I needed to grow. I didn't fear judgment by using these terms. I was trusting my therapist that I could actually use these new words so I could express how I felt, and these were <u>my</u> words; they expressed feelings that no one could take away. Learning to use these new descriptive words that were once blocked from my vocabulary in proper context, that could now help me express myself and my experience, was freeing.

CHAPTER SEVEN

Unjustified Shame and Guilt, and Learning to Use Corrective Information

Here is where I began to learn more about unjustified shame and guilt. The DBT skill, Opposite Action, along with corrective information, are extremely important to know and to learn how to incorporate into daily life. It is also crucial to distinguish the difference between justified and unjustified feelings of guilt and/or shame, since those feelings can often trip up many of us.

I twisted everything into feeling shameful or guilty. I was once told that I was wired "emotionally sensitive," which actually is very true, as I am very driven by emotional stimuli. That is only the beginning. We all need to be aware that our emotions have also been influenced or shaped by our life experiences, including society and family environments. Shame has been a very destructive emotion for me, especially as I learned that many of my beliefs were or are unjustified feelings of shame and guilt. I feel that, for many years, I misinterpreted the difference between justified and unjustified. I let shame and guilt rule my existence. I never realized how destructive that was. I believed I was bad, a failure, and so on. In addition, the feeling of guilt and shame influenced the creation of my negative thoughts, which fueled my ongoing negative self-talk (that record that never stopped).

I was constantly ruminating on what a failure I was, including the thoughts of embarrassment and needing to hide. It wasn't until Neal challenged my thoughts and showed me first the difference between shame and guilt and then how to acknowledge the difference between justified and unjustified shame and guilt.

I looked up the word "shame," and I found it means, "believing you are bad or do not amount to much as a human being." (dictionary.com) Looking through my journals from 20 years ago, I found this picture, along with a poem I wrote back when I was very anorexic. When I was malnourished, it was not uncommon for me to have such negative thoughts, which was like a broken record playing in my head. It was about how I felt when I looked into the mirror, I saw no identity. Below is that journal entry, I call it "Identity crisis."

My reflection

I see nothing empty & plain

dispensable

frustration sets in

my reflection

I see fat ugliness and despair

anger enters

searching for answers

searching for truth

I weigh myself

My reflection

confirmed hopeless

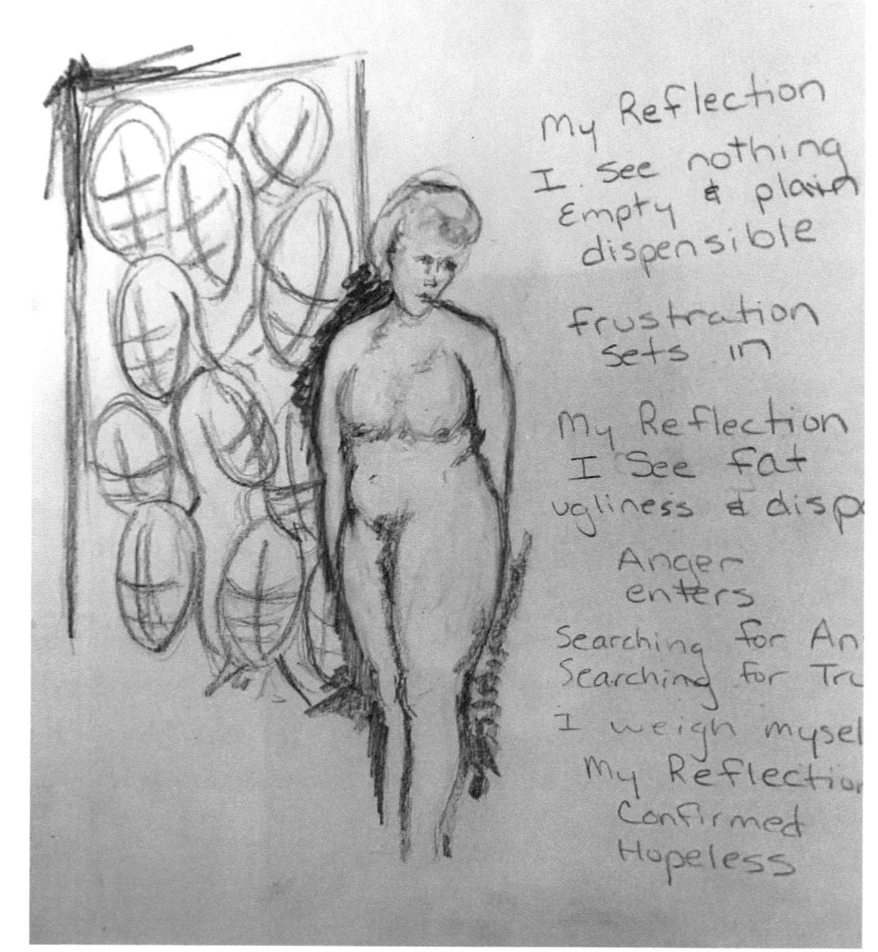

I often believed that people hated me, and had the fear that they might abandon me. I had to challenge these old beliefs and to see for myself that this was unjustified shame.

Shame is justified when you do something wrong or offensive to someone, and they may choose not to be friends with you any longer. *Unjustified* shame means that these thoughts are not true, and the fears of being left aside or hated by your friend may not be reality. I learned that these negative thoughts were driven by beliefs and myths from my past life experiences.

The same goes for unjustified guilt, which has led me to unnecessary pain, suffering, and self-hate. An example of guilt is when your actions or behaviors are against your own values or moral code.

If one believes in unjustified shame and/or guilt, but the beliefs are not reality, then the beliefs become ineffective, except to cause self-loathing and/or self-hate. I often twisted my thoughts and, without checking the facts of the situation, I would turn my feelings into shame and guilt. This only led me down a path of more anxiety, in addition to relying on unhealthy coping mechanisms. I now realize the importance of looking at my thoughts and what triggers them. This really gave me an opportunity to slow down and see what was justified and unjustified. This was extremely helpful to get me out of the black hole of existence.

As I began to radically accept that many of my thoughts were unjustified, I was taught how to apply another DBT skill: *Opposite Action*. This skill was crucial, as it helped me to effectively regulate my emotions.

Before I could take this step toward Opposite Action, I had to see which of my beliefs and thoughts fit the facts. I had to identify the emotion and its action urge. I then learned that many of my beliefs or thoughts of myself didn't fit the facts—they were unjustified. This unjustified shame or guilt had no real reason other than to bring me to more pain and suffering. I was able to see that I created these thoughts, which were often fueled by my eating disorder-thinking. What I needed to do was just the opposite of what I was thinking. You see, when guilt or shame are not justified, you have to re-learn that these thoughts are not effective and can become harmful.

I began to list of some of my beliefs on shame and guilt—the *myths* that I believed. These beliefs ran wild in my head, which is often referred to as a "trance-like thinking" (term coined by Tara Brach). Everything that happened was my fault which fueled guilt, along with being ashamed of the way I looked (this was just another eating disorder thought being fueled). I was constantly degrading myself. Then, as I relooked at everything, using corrective information and facts, I **STOPPED** (remembering the DBT skill, S.T.O.P.). I **T**ook a step back and breathed, and **O**bserved the negative thoughts, and **P**roceeded mindfully. This is when I could move into the skill, Opposite Action.

Opposite Action

A person needs to slow down so they can be mindful, which allows them to notice the thoughts and emotions, and the subsequent action urge. Here is where you acknowledge your emotion, then check the facts to see if they are justified or unjustified.

Prior to DBT, I would just stuff my emotions, or didn't even recognize them, as I turned to my eating disorder to avoid any and all emotions at all costs. I was finally learning that I truly was feeling and that I did have these emotions but had been suppressing them for so long. I had to learn to acknowledge I had feelings, not to suppress these emotions (especially shame and guilt). Suppressing my emotions only created unhealthy urges, and compulsively triggered poor choices.

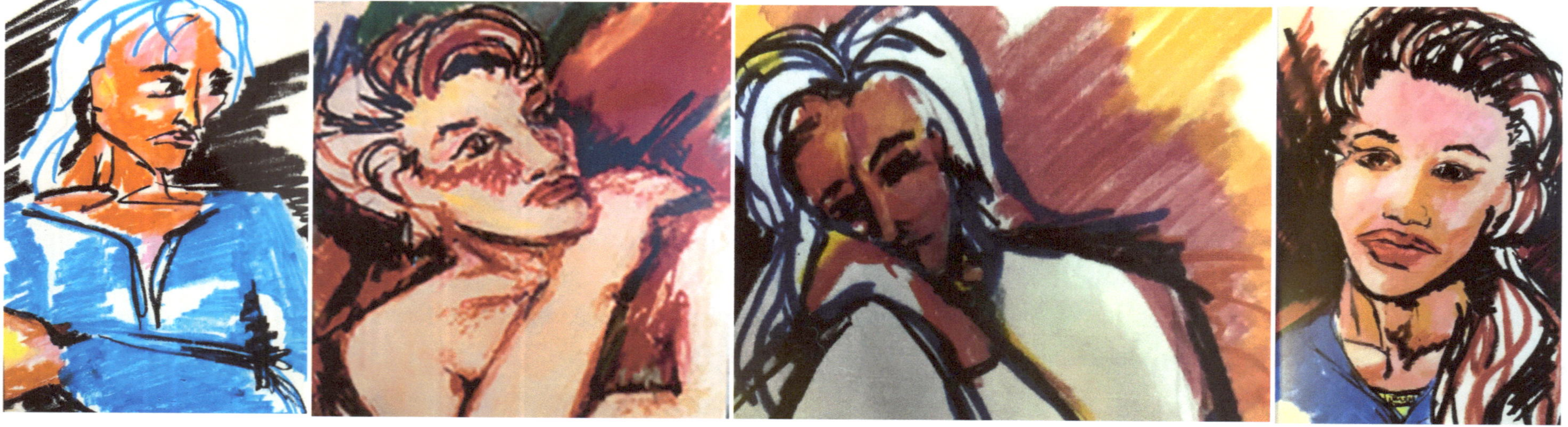

By learning DBT skills, acknowledging my feelings, and getting in touch with these emotions, I was able to get in touch with my feelings of shame, which I learned were not justified. When I checked the facts of my experience, I could see and accept that I did nothing wrong, it was the perpetrator who did wrong—not me—it was him. This brought me to the real feelings I was having, one of which I never knew I had inside me: ANGER.

These drawings were done with oil pastels. I started out with the feeling I had at that moment, anger. I never really knew how to feel angry. I'm still working on how to process anger to this day. There's a purpose behind every emotion.

I needed to process these feelings, check the facts, and then work through the information in a healthy, coping way. My best way of coping is to turn to drawing.

The first drawing above is me, in my feelings of anger and stubbornness. I quickly moved into shame followed by sadness. The last pastel drawing was me learning, which I now understand was me taking care of and nurturing myself. To me it has a look of understanding and compassion. It's calmer than the first "angry" picture. I mentioned earlier, I never thought I had anger. Well, I do, and that is okay—what I do with it is the important thing. I need to process it—not to turn it inwards toward myself—acknowledge my emotion, place it where it belongs, and learn from it as I move forward using the skills I was taught.

That was me identifying that, *yes, I was angry*, not at myself, but at the perpetrator. This then led to another feeling: sadness. I was being overwhelmed initially by all these feelings that normally I blocked out. I needed to learn the purpose of these emotions and that they helped me to problem-solve. For example, being angry at the perpetrator helped me resolve that my anger was justified, and he was the bad person, he was the perpetrator who was trying to control and destroy my life. It took my Art Therapy and working through my DBT skills with my therapist to learn how to feel anger, and where the true anger belonged. "Feeling the feels" had a whole new meaning. I began to understand and accept my experience. I don't have to like what happened, but I do have to radically accept in this present moment that it *did happen*. This allowed me to see my anger, and to place the anger where it belonged.

I now look at the sketches and I am sad for myself, that I had for such a long time kept my pain and suffering a secret. I see now that I benefited by speaking up and telling my story. Once I acknowledged my experience, and shared it with my therapist, the true learning began. I could challenge myths and some of my negative thinking. It was then I could work on using and allowing myself to see the corrective information. This information taught me the purpose of my emotions and to get in touch with my emotions; to see that my anger was justified. This let me let go of shame and move forward. As I write this book, I am still learning one of the most important and final pieces to my recovery: how to radically accept something from my past for what it was, and then provide myself the nurturing compassion I need in the present.

I really want to take this moment to share and thank the mastermind of DBT, Marsha Linehan. I feel I need to share this extraordinary woman's creation of DBT. She lived a life creating, and personally using, each and every skill to live a life worth living. She was so determined to not only teach people about DBT, but also help others to get out of hell and experience a life worth living.

Marsha Linehan is internationally known for her work. I am so thankful for her work and her life's experiences. I believe in her work. My goal is to bring her work, along with my experience and passion for art, with the help of my therapist, together as I share my journey of health and longevity. I want to follow in her footsteps, by telling my story so I can demonstrate how effective DBT skills are and why they should be available for everyone to use. The trend now is to have a DBT unit geared to, and available for, school-aged children. There are now new programs developing in schools as well as for adults working through their own experiences.

The following are just some of the DBT skills that I have incorporated into my life, and as you go through the rest of this book you'll see how my artwork helped me to break down some of the skills to provide a better understanding of how I can incorporate them into my life.

I had to ask myself if the emotion was justified, and if the intensity of the emotion was justified or helpful. If the emotion was not justified, or the intensity of the emotion was not helpful, my next step would move me to the skill of Opposite Action of the emotional urge.

Looking back through this process, I held on to what happened for a long time. Holding in all these thoughts just created the pain within me, and the feelings of shame and guilt. Then those beliefs fueled my eating disorder which grew into shame of how I looked. All this is what led up to my constant negative self-talk.

The sketches on page 76 remind me of all this negative self-talk and a very difficult time in my life. As I look back at my journals and see these sketches, I am reminded of how painful life was when I misinterpreted my emotions and believed they were justified. This misunderstanding and not having the DBT skills are why all my sketches depicted my self-hate. It was a terrible way to live, and to feel about myself. I created a life of fear and loneliness because I was always in my head, constantly battling these negative thoughts.

After I had a better understanding of justified and unjustified emotions, Neal introduced me to a yet another new tool called *Corrective Information*. Sometimes when you have an automatic response to think or say something negative about yourself, you need to S.T.O.P., take a step back, observe what's going on and what triggered these thoughts, and proceed mindfully. Then with the corrective information, I was learning to let go of the negative thought and give myself some compassion.

My work on corrective information often taught me to put new light on what I was thinking. For example, if my thought was, *I am a fat, lazy slob* (yet another thought constantly driven by my eating disorder), I might look at what really triggered that thought, then replace it with many of my positive attributes that describe me from within. I often relied on what was positive in my life, such as my feelings about how I raised my boys, the love I shared with my husband, and my whole family, or my love for helping individuals with disabilities. I was so quick to judge myself or think negatively when all I had to do was look at what was right in front of me. This was when I began to acknowledge what was my corrective information. I worked on using these tools and skills to learn to rebuild a positive self-image and self-acceptance. This helped to remove any unjustified feelings of shame and judgement and to look at what I have conquered from within. Utilizing corrective information was a big piece of my journey, and a new outlook for me. This tool took me to the level of intensity I needed to challenge and conquer the negative beliefs I carried for years.   The following picture and phrases reminded me to accept what is, and to let go of unnecessary negative thoughts. This picture is pasted to the bottom of my bathroom mirror. As part of my morning routine, when I look into the mirror, I am always reminded of where I was and where I am, and that I am brave, I am resilient, and I am beautiful inside and out.

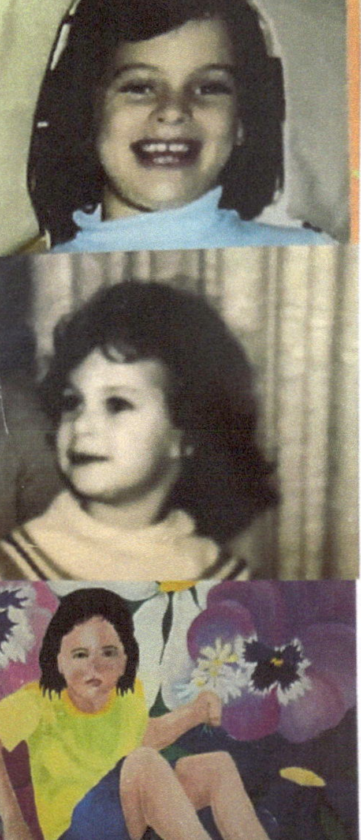

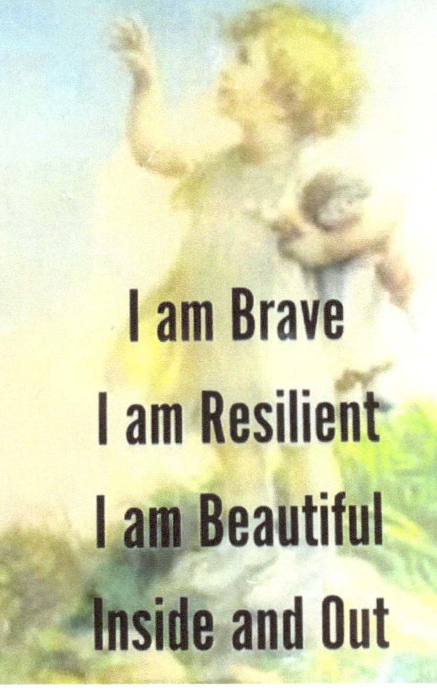

Corrective Information

The following pieces of artwork were from a time of my life where I was very underweight. I called it my "black and white" stage of life. I was so malnourished that I could not see any color. My brain was starving and unable to process information. My drawings became nothing more than black and white sketches. As time went on, the drawings regressed to being very childlike and nothing like my past artwork.

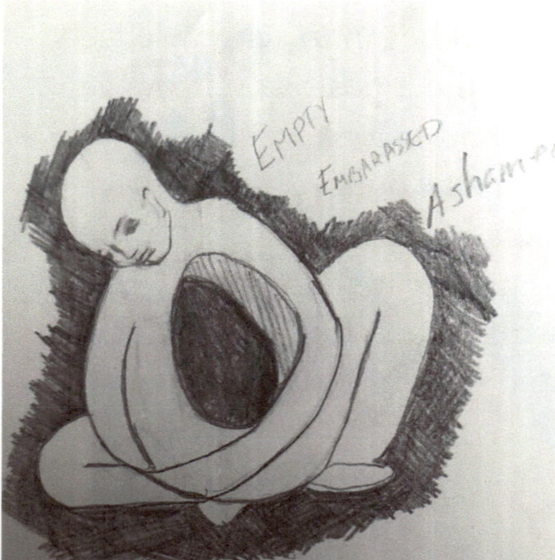

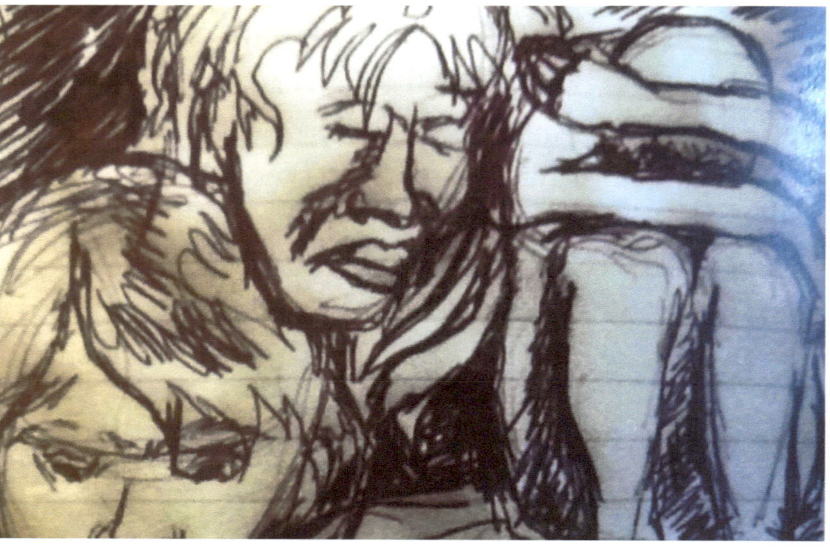

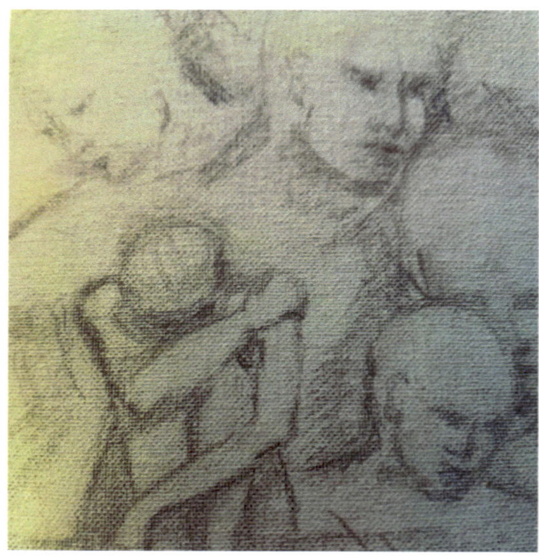

This also was the time in my life in which I lived every moment in fear. I had such extreme feelings of fear that I felt I could die. I had fears of losing something or someone very important to me. Fear not only plagued me during the day, but my nights were filled with nightmares. I found myself screaming in silence in the middle of the night, or filled with nightmares of being harmed or traumatized. I had such fear of being attacked while sleeping, I would hold on to myself for protection from the torment of fear that I experienced.

This fear led to other interpretations, such as fear related to being rejected, criticized, or embarrassing myself. I felt like I had to be on the lookout, I wanted to scream but most of the time I was frozen from fear, and my screams were silent.

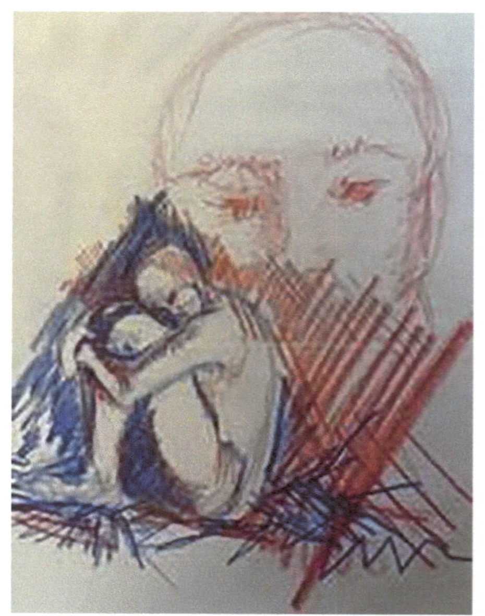

Silenced

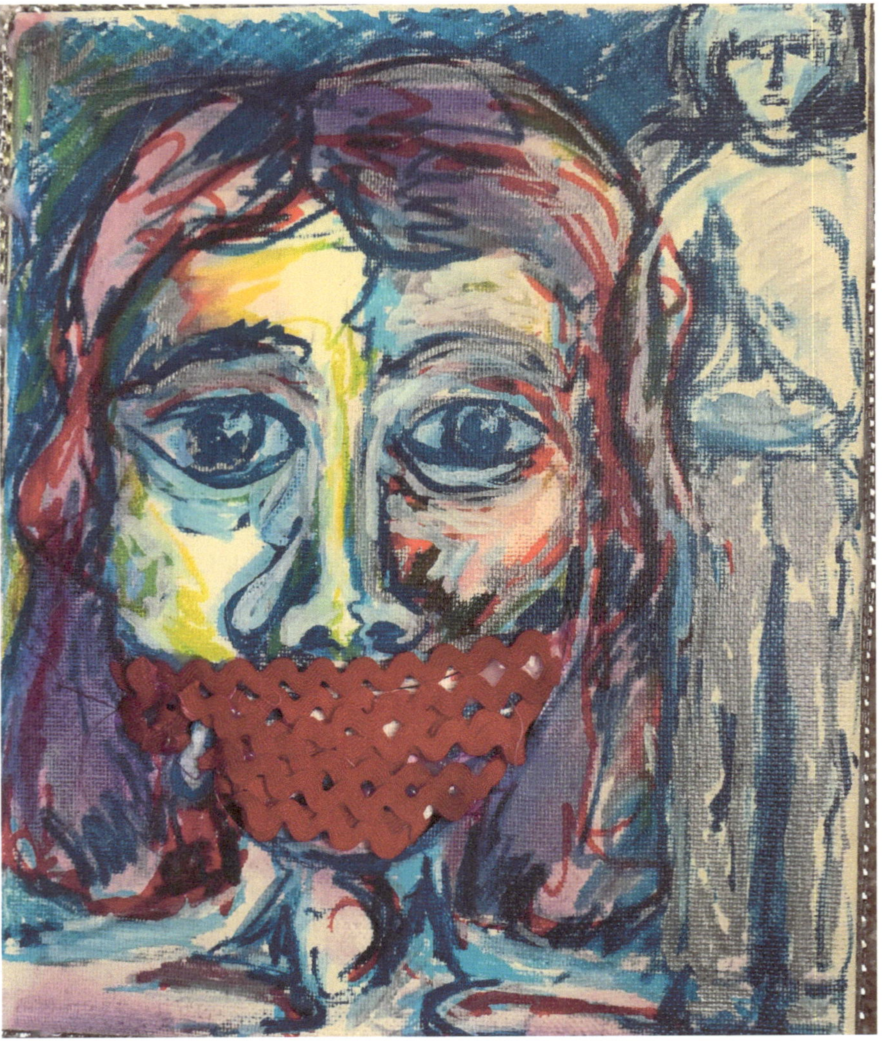

This piece of artwork shows how the DBT sessions were teaching me how to acknowledge and get in touch with my feelings. *Silenced* represented my pain and suffering I was feeling at the time. My sessions with Neal gave me the skills to see how out of touch I was and not connected to my feelings. *Silenced* also shows my anger and sadness, related to how the case was finally settled. Many might say I won, but to me, with the gag order still in place, I feel there is some unfinished business, especially when I want to cry out with pain. The tears in this piece have so much more power to me, because I was learning how to feel, and that allowed me access to my tears. For many years my tears never came, now they are more available as I feel sadness. First guilt, shame, then anger—but most importantly, the sadness. The sadness was my own validation of the horror I experienced, and it also showed me that I came to radical acceptance of what happened. It does not say I accept or even forgive. It says I radically accept *that it happened*; that was then, and now I am in a safe place. *Silenced* helped me to process the reality of what I was learning with the DBT skills. It helped me see where the blame should go, and also helped me to validate my experience. This experience has definitely affected my life: yet with my family by my side, and the help from Neal and Dr. Laura, and as DBT and my Art came together, I made leaps and bounds in my recovery.

I am thankful for Neal pushing me through this experience and creating a safety zone for me to walk thru and helping me to process my feelings. *YES*; I found out, through all this work with Neal and Dr. Laura, I truly had feelings. What the heck, I remember for years I sat face to face with Dr. Laura denying that there was an angry bone in me. Yet when it finally came out, I was like, *wow, it's been there all this time*. As Dr. Laura explained that was where my eating disorder came into play. So for everyone out there, *Yes, I do have feelings; we all have feelings, and our feelings have a purpose*. Dr. Laura broke down how and why, all these years, I used my eating disorder (which almost killed me), instead of feeling my feelings, expressing my emotions. At one point, Dr. Laura was helping me to see how my art was actually expressing my feelings which I just couldn't find the words for at the time. I found it very helpful to process my art and how it connected to what I was learning with Neal. Together I pushed through my therapy sessions with Neal and explored the role of my eating disorder with Dr. Laura. I finally was in touch with insight of how I was crying for help, expressing my needs, and telling my story, with my art. Then the skills I was learning helped me walk my journey, to knock down my fears, and find my voice. Art Therapy helped me to feel and to see that all along I really was this strong, loving, courageous woman. This was my identity, not my eating disorder or my trauma. It was my art, along with my new DBT skills that became my tools to express myself when I felt I had no words available.

I know that I was justified to have a lot of negative thoughts, but put in perspective, if I want to heal, I need to look at corrective information. The following piece talks about loss, but looking closer at the words, corrective information is there.

Tear of Shame

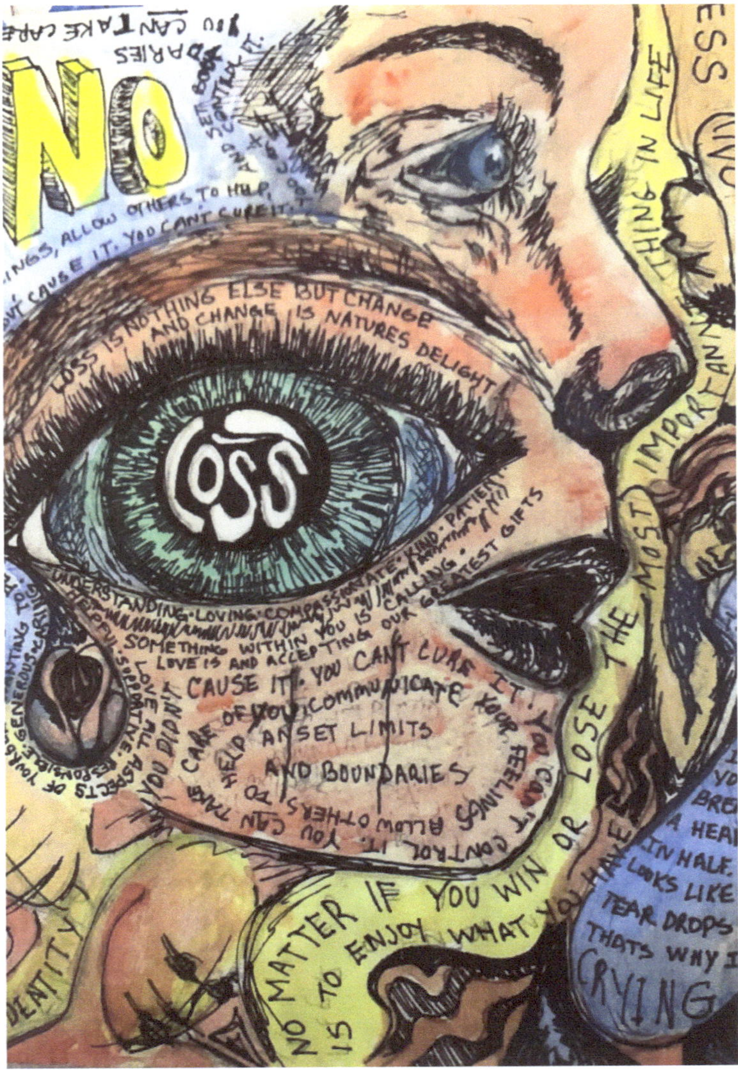

I am using the above drawing to follow the importance of mindfulness, as well as breaking down some of the components of the drawing itself. There are many places in this book where I could use this drawing—it covers so many areas of growth along the way of my journey. It is centered on *loss*. When I first began sharing, and opening up to Neal,

I always zoomed in and kept my focus on all that I lost because of the abuse. I believed when this all happened, I was at the height of my career. I was awarded Wisconsin Art Teacher of the Year, Wisconsin Bell teacher of the year, I traveled and spoke all over the U.S. and in England…. The list went on, but what Neal pointed out was, while I may have won these awards, it was at that time when my eating disorder was controlling my life. So maybe if I relooked at this time of my life, I was vulnerable, and easy prey to a predator. I look deeper into the sketch and see three tear drops. One tear drop embodied a person full of shame, covering her head as if to hide from the world. Another tear drop talks about "if you break my heart in two you have two tear drops, that's because I am crying." I focused on pain, loss, and crying, yet my eating disorder kept me so numb, I never felt those tears. I drew empty faces—no features, no eyes, nose, or mouth. This was because I felt I had no identity. So here I push my level of work to success, yet I didn't know my true self. The pain was my loss. There is so much in this one sketch; for example, my decline in development and the loss of control to my predator. I was becoming detached from the world around me.

This painting, *Optimistic,* was done on a 4 x 4½-foot canvas. When you walk into the room where it hangs, you need to study the colors and angles. I was truly mindful as I worked on this piece, completely focusing on this painting. I had just had a good week, working with corrective information whenever I was challenged with negativity or an urge to act out. This focus was in the moment, and I was in tune to how I was feeling. This painting represented my growth in finding myself and some of the old confidence I had before my trauma and my eating disorder took over.

I was getting my confidence back, and I was excited to try to tackle this large-sized canvas. I'd never tried anything this big before, nor had I painted anything with this much expression or life. With my DBT skills, I was able to not just try, but take action and accomplish what I set out to do.

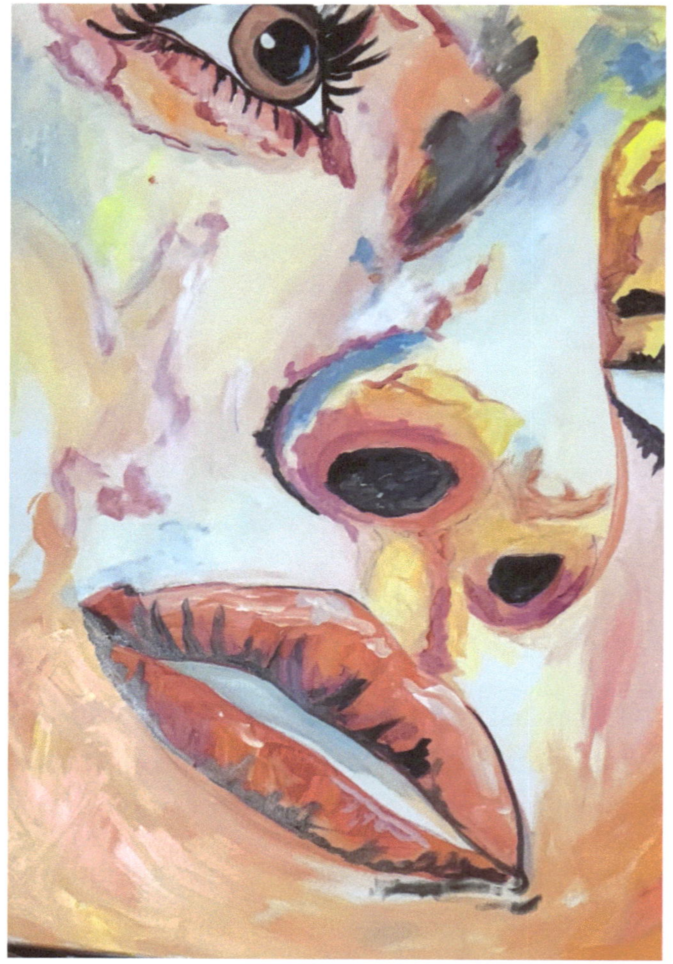

Optimistic

CHAPTER EIGHT

My *Woman* Series

The **Woman** series represents several stages I went through while I was totally consumed by my eating disorder.

Depression

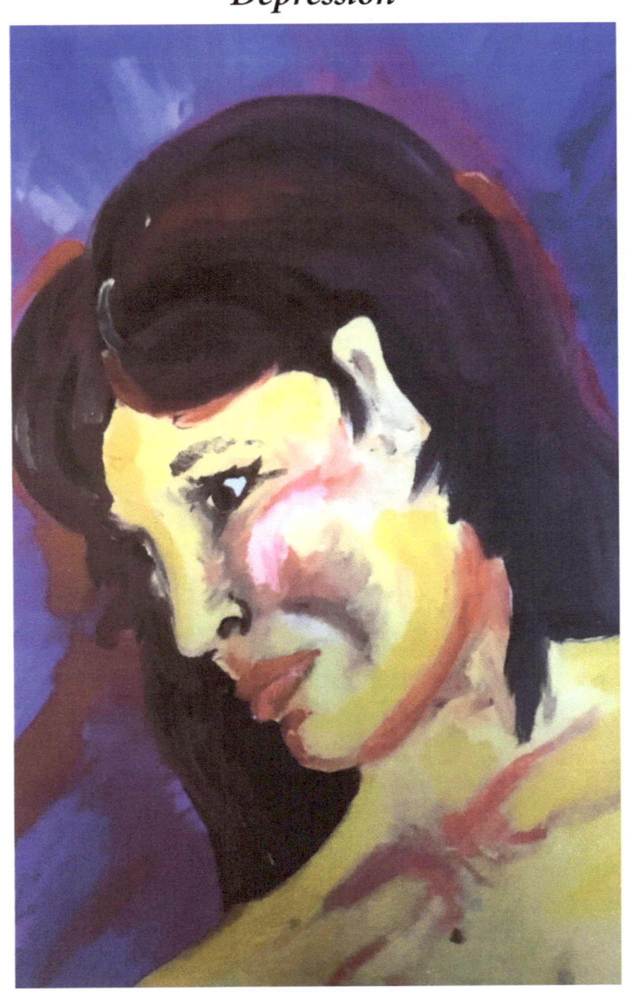

The first picture represents the stage where my eating disorder had affected me so much that I could hardly take care of myself. It was also when people were trying to convince me I had an eating disorder, but I was in denial, and feeling everyone was against me. I had fallen into a debilitating form of depression. I truly believed, in the beginning, that my secret diet was my power and that it was what energized me. I later learned my eating disorder became my "love-hate relationship" that played games with my thoughts and interpretations. I was getting sicker, and the eating disorder consumed 100% of my day by filling my day with more rules, rituals, and beliefs I had to follow. What I didn't realize was the disease was swallowing me whole. I never saw the real life stressors and emotions I was hiding from. It was this painting that represented the stage that this so-called power of mine turned south, because along with the eating disorder I became majorly depressed. My husband and my boys were what kept me alive. There was a time I felt swallowed up, suffocating in my own negative thinking. I was once this very accomplished and effective administrator, who loved providing opportunities for individuals with disabilities. Then as I entered the world of a life-threatening eating disorder, combined with depression, I was what they called a "revolving door patient," in and out of inpatient care. I was drowning, lifeless, over-medicated; a blank face.

Unattainable

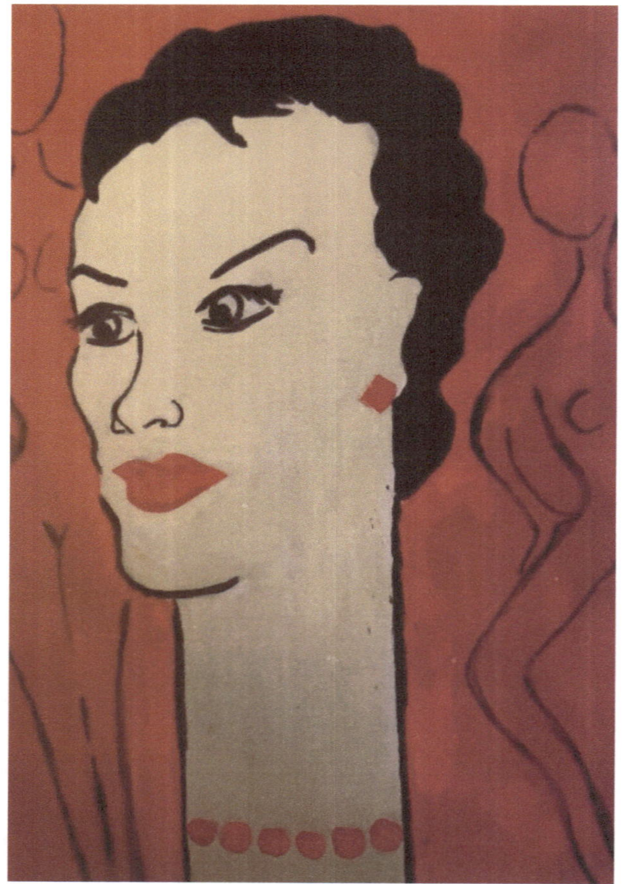

This picture was another example of how I believed society viewed women. An eating disorder may not develop necessarily by society alone. Yet for those who are sensitive to such perceived standards, expectations just might internalize such judgement. The media, and the photoshopping of models, was regularly done to make them look a certain way, which was definitely not realistic. These images helped millions of individuals go on diets after diets. Some young girls only dreamt of these idolized images. Many young women, when at this vulnerable age, would go to extremes such as having surgeries, to conform to these unnatural standards. When I was at this age, these images in magazines and other advertisements drove my need to succeed and to be the best. I would also twist positive comments into my own negative self-talk, a bad habit I developed along with my poor self-image.

Women were only to be looked at, often seen as objects or sexualized. Women were supposed to be quiet and stand aside. That was many years ago, and fortunately times have changed a bit in some of these areas. I can see growth and more awareness and a stronger fight for women to be able to reach their dreams and succeed.

Asking for Help

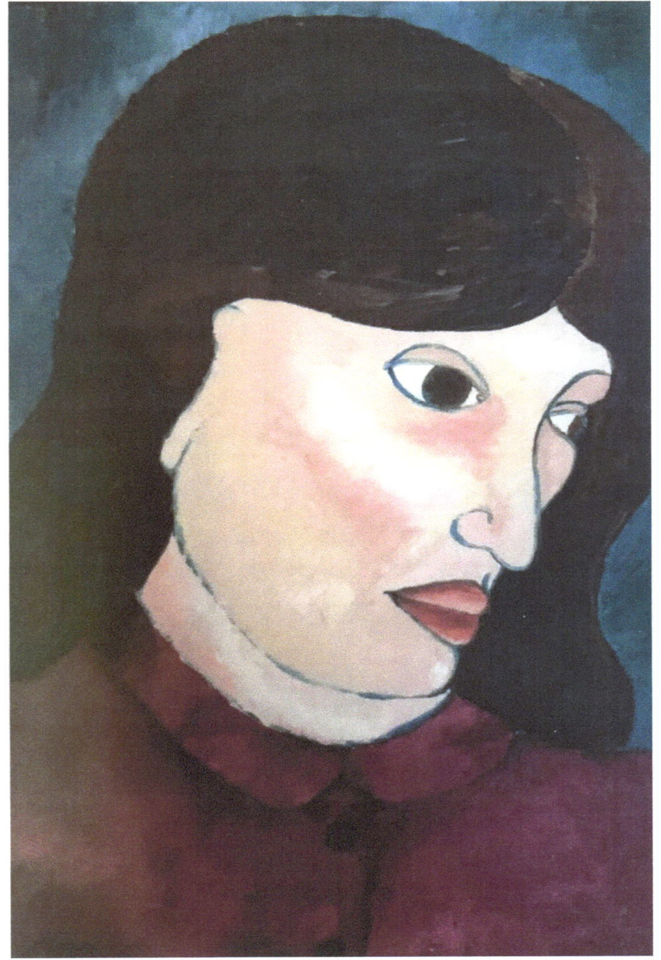

The third picture in the series is where I began to realize I needed help. I learned later, in DBT, that the skill I was using was called, "**turning the mind**." It's when I finally chose between staying on the path of suffering or the path of health. I eventually, after years of suffering, could see I was living a life of fear. Every aspect of my life was based on fear. Fear of food, rejection, my weight, abandonment, failure, and being judged (which usually meant I was assuming or predicting what someone was thinking about me, which may not have been reality). When I experienced my trauma, the list of fear-based thinking became insurmountable. I had what Neal called "safety checks." I constantly would look out the windows and doors of my home for signs of danger. Every sound I heard, I would panic that something was wrong or someone was going to come hurt me and my family. My biggest fears were manifested from my own thinking. So often I would twist comments into something very negative. I needed to step back and realize that the bottom line was **I was fearful and avoiding being in touch with my emotions**. I did not know how to deal with my emotions. I needed to ask for help. I wanted to move on with my life. This led me to learning one of the basic skills of DBT, aimed towards **core mindfulness**. Core mindfulness is the foundation of DBT. Mindfulness is when one is aware of one's own thoughts, feelings, behaviors, and behavioral urges. As I painted, I was aware, that for me to understand myself I had to accept myself, as well as change some of my beliefs and behaviors. For me to reach out for help and to learn how to get out of my own head was to practice three skills of mindfulness: to **observe, describe**, and then **participate** in my journey to health and of radical acceptance. To observe is to notice what is happening, such as my thoughts and body sensations, and to just "watch it." Then, I learned how to describe what was happening in the present moment, no matter how distressing it was. Generally, I would have a thought or body sensation (pounding heart, sweaty palms, etc.) and react to it impulsively. Being so impulsive kept me from learning that, instead of reacting negatively, I could actually survive my feelings by learning to ride the wave and seeing that I would be safe—that nothing catastrophic would happen.

When Neal was teaching me how to *ride the wave*, and what the term meant in my journey, I was grasping at the concept. In the first version of this painting, I put splashing waves, thinking I knew what he meant. But as we worked harder on my experiences that were more intense, I realized I needed a more intense wave.

This painting was hanging in Neal's office, and he took it off the wall and said, "When you are ready to ride the wave of the intensity of your emotions, I'll put this back up." He continued to explain that the work I was doing was a lot more intense than when I was first introduced to *riding the wave*. He said, "You need to meet it with the same intensity."

"You need a new wave, a tsunami wave."

I did a second version of the painting with that tsunami, and I put *everything* into it, I even put my brushes down and got my hands into it. Then I understood what Neal was saying.

There is an obvious difference between these two waves. As I was painting the second one, I felt every single body sensation, the intensity that we were talking about. Even the colors were more intense. And I learned that I survived the tsunami. I believe the two paintings show a progression of my therapy and my journey.

Riding the Wave (versions 1 and 2)

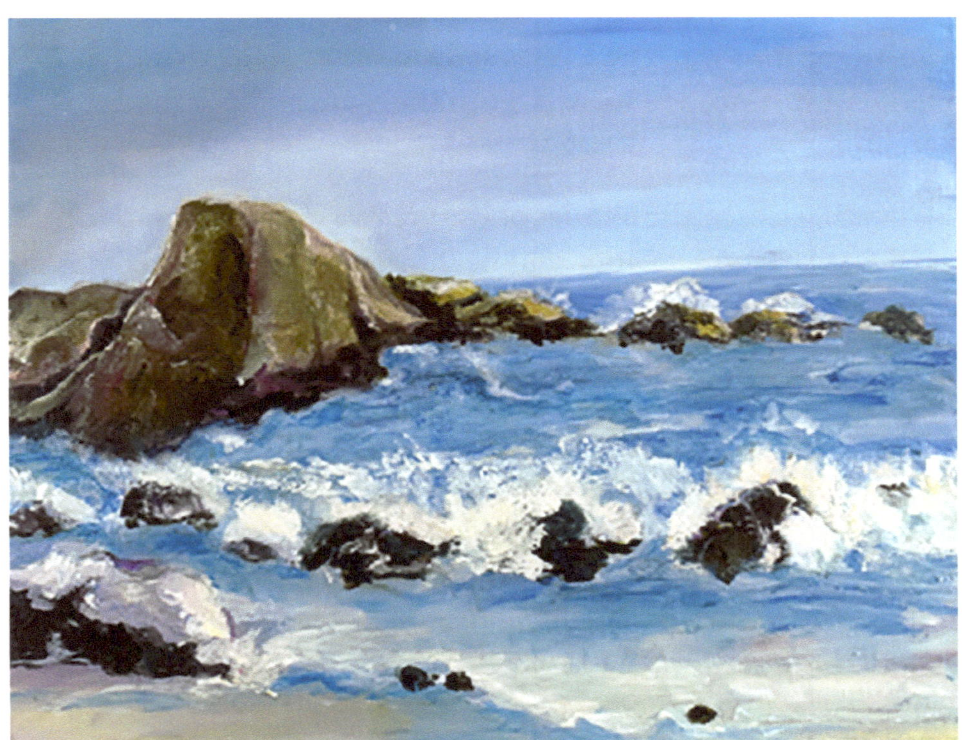

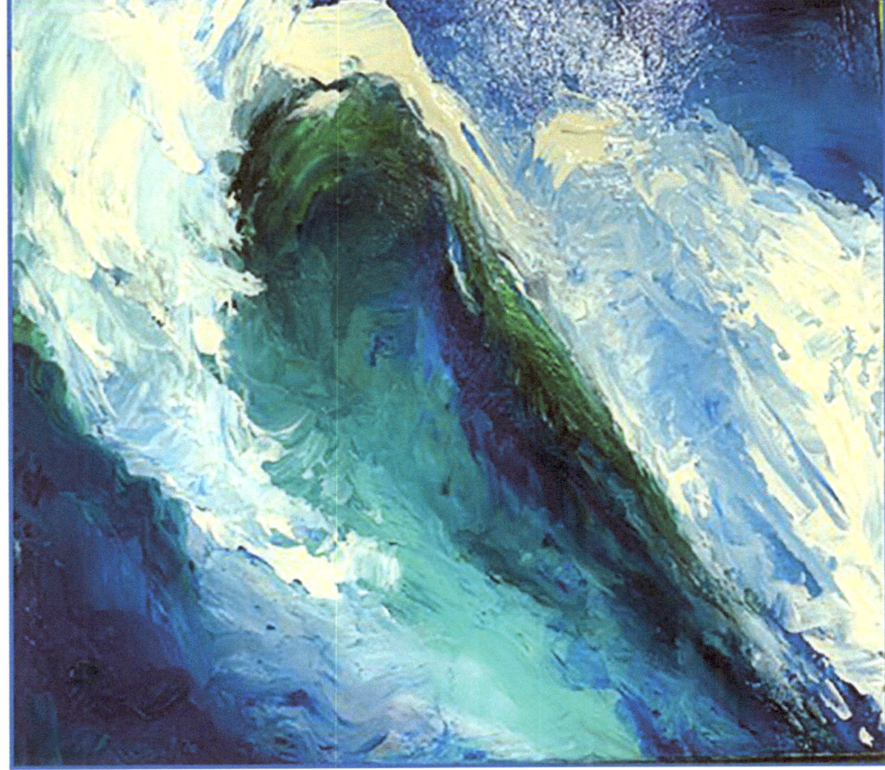

Finally the third mindfulness skill I was learning was to participate, and participate fully. The skill is, when you decide to participate, you have to do it all the way. To do whatever it is you're doing, be mindful and focus on it and commit to it. I truly believe this painting was saying I was ready to be mindful, and I was ready to observe, describe, and participate with everything I had to succeed at a life worth living. I just needed to step up to the plate and ask for help.

Beauty

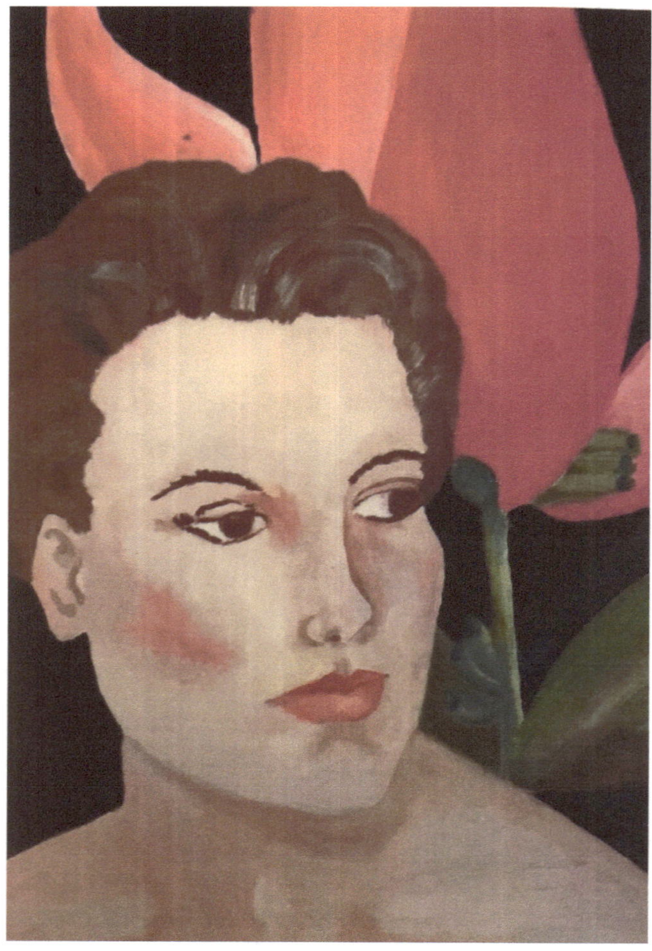

Back to the *Woman* series…The picture of *Beauty* was my representation of what I believed was strength, beauty, and health. To me, my mother was the epitome of beauty, strength, and health, both inside and out. I remember my mom always wearing her hair up in a bun. I remember her being so strong, and for fighting for what she believed in. My Mom was always there for all her children. When I started this painting, I didn't intend to actually paint a portrait of her, but to paint the beauty of her. I chose to place a flower behind her because it too was beautiful, and gardening was very much what my mother loved to do. I wanted this painting to be everything that was my mother. My mother represented beauty to me because she had the whole package. She was beautiful, lovable, and happy with herself and who she was. She was extremely happy with the love of her life, and my father loved her just the same. My parents meant everything to me. They are now together in heaven. I miss their presence; I miss so much about them. Yet knowing that they are together and watching over us all makes me smile. I still remember my father's last words to my mom, "I love you forever," and that he did. I believe my mom knew she was a very good mother, and I also recall her saying to me once, "I did the best I could with what I had." She loved all of her children. There were no judgments from our parents; they accepted us for who we were and always saw the good in every one of us. So, when I say my mother was my idol of beauty, she really was, inside and out.

As you can see, I adored my parents. They were amazing. They taught my siblings and me how to love one another. I also learned from them that beauty comes from your values and morals in life. My mother saw the best in everyone, and she taught me to live by my heart, and more importantly to accept the differences of others, while seeing the beauty in that. She stood tall and strong. I believe my parents loved me for me. So, this painting is important to my *Woman* series because it was a goal of mine to be very much like my mother. I thought the cards I was dealt, including my traumatic experience which I would never wish on anyone, put me far from my goal. I realize now, many years after these paintings, that I *am* reaching my goal. The goal was always there…I was my mother in many ways. It took me to be willing to jump on the right path; to be willing to work with my treatment team; to feed my brain; to learn new skills from my therapist, Neal, and from the DBT program; and then to use my art skills to process it all. This was when so many of the pieces began to fit. Yes, the goal was to be like my mother, and to be loved by both my mother and father. But then the answer came: the main person I needed to be loved and accepted by was *myself*…that is <u>beauty</u>.

Unfinished Journey

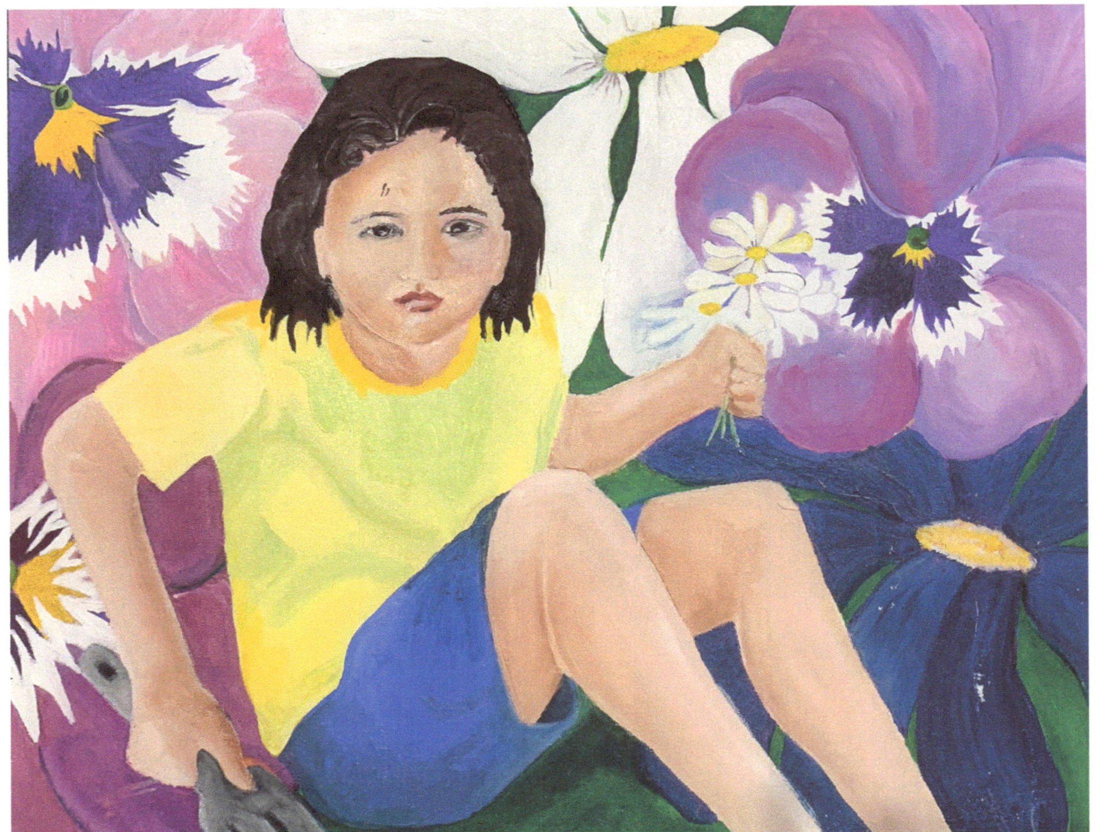

The *Woman* series was painted many years ago. Back then, I truly believed I was on my way to success, and my journey of dealing with my eating disorder was over. So, I painted this little girl digging in the garden of flowers; it represented my inner child surrounded by all the flowers that were blooming. At the time I was painting, I thought I was her. Now, looking back, I understand why I never finished this painting. It was as if my art knew my journey wasn't even close to the end—I only had a few pieces of the puzzle and a lot of learning to do. This realization came to me when I was introduced to my DBT therapist.

Initially, when I began my work with Neal, he scared me. As time moved on, I was learning the skills of DBT to the point I was hungry to learn more. I didn't fear Neal anymore because I felt he was my lifeline to being healthy. Neal is knowledgeable and his passion is to educate his clients to want to apply their new skills into their everyday experiences. He wants to teach his clients that *living* means to live life as an exposure, to do it over and over until you learn from it.

So back to my unfinished painting. Back when I started painting it, I really believed I was cured from my eating disorder. Then when I looked back and saw I never finished it, I could see it was just another step in my time line. My art documented my life's journey. This was my timeline, my journey. My health.

I added *Let it Be* to the collection. This painting is set in the fall, my favorite season, when my father and I would drive for hours to see the colors on the trees. It illustrates the tree of life and the tree of family in the side of the face (my face), and I am blowing the negative thoughts and memories away, and they turn into doves. That is my way of saying, *let it go and let it be.*

Let it Be

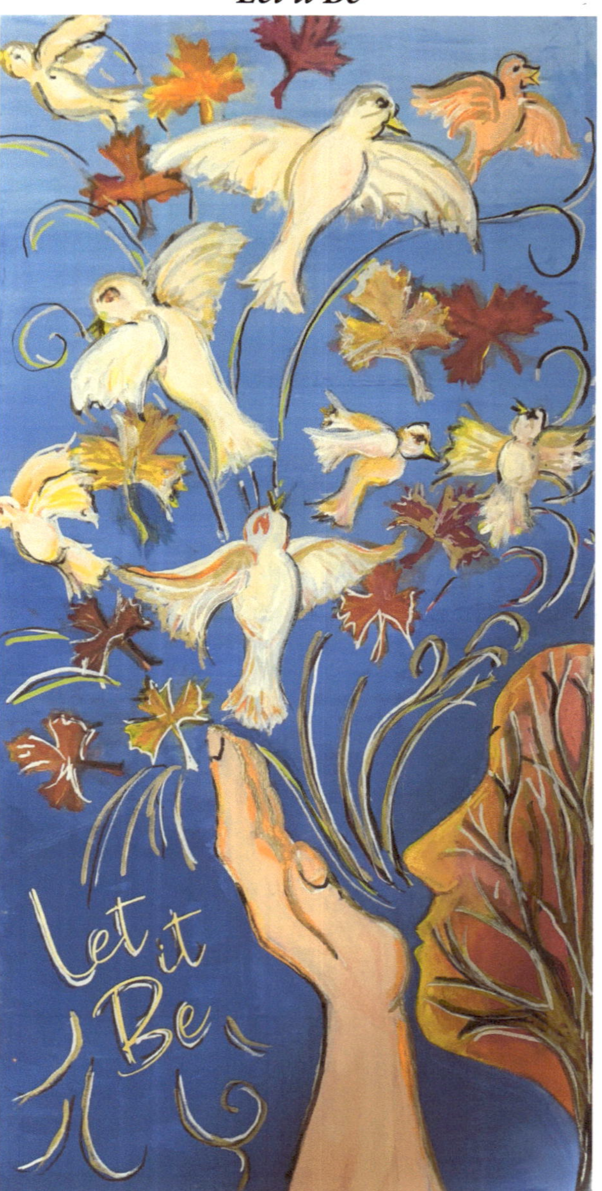

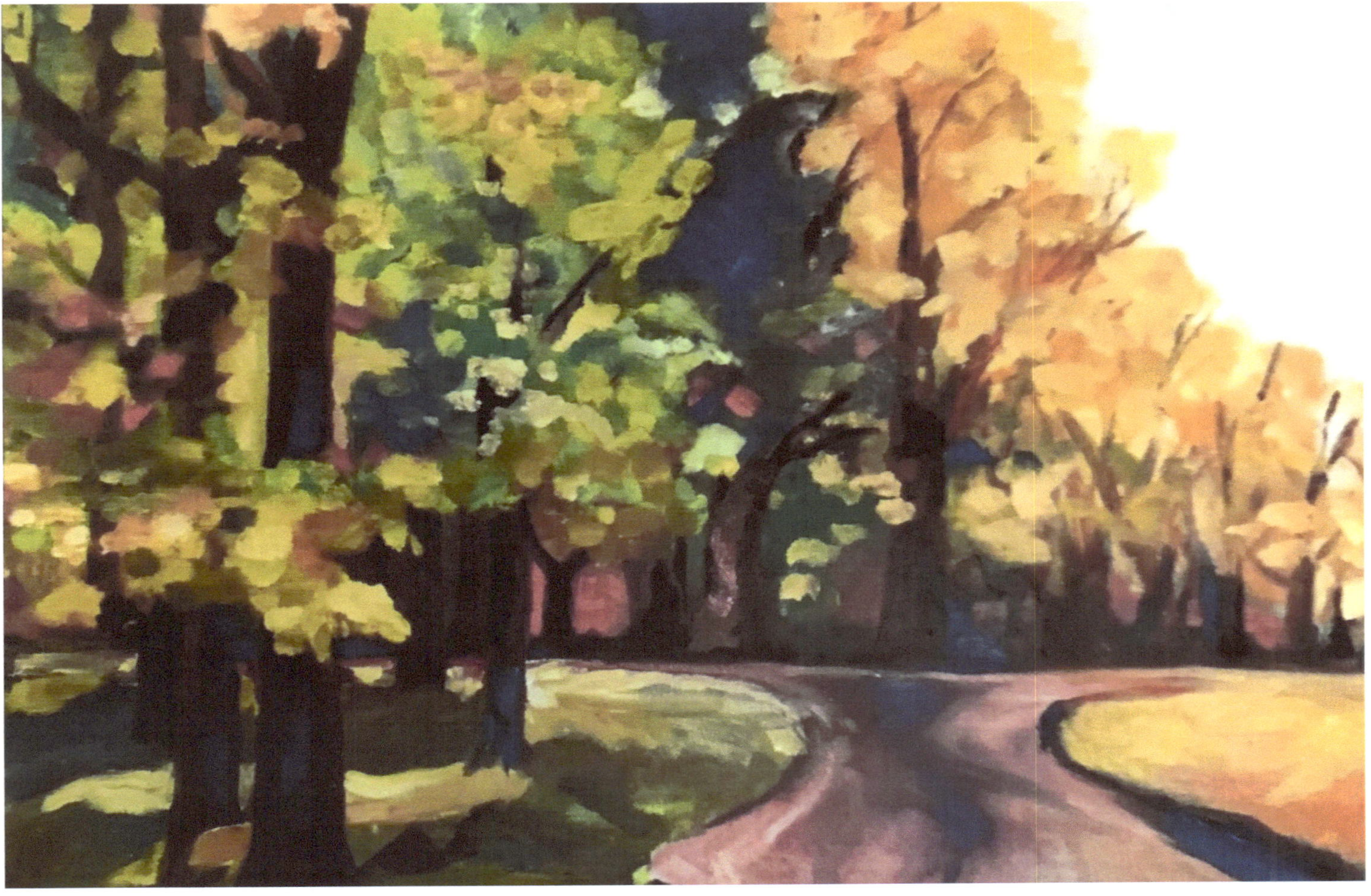

It was here when I realized I had so few skills to get me through this; so the real journey began. I believe the beginning of my journey was to get me re-fed and get my brain working again. It was this time that my art could help me break down what I was learning in the DBT, and cognitively I began to understand how the skills could help me. I developed a strong sense of hope.

Many years later, with the help of both Neal and Dr. Laura, and a lot of hard work, I finished the following painting. It began as the subject of sharing my life with my older sister. She was always my flower child, and so free. When I started the painting, it was to be of my sister as the nurturing adult and me as the child; then I realized that I was a lot like my sister—loving—so I was both the woman *and* the child. I added it to my *Woman* series. It was when I painted this painting, *Strong, Loving, Courageous Woman*, I knew I'd turned the corner. I was ready to take the next step to self-acceptance, and self-love.

Strong, Loving, Courageous Woman

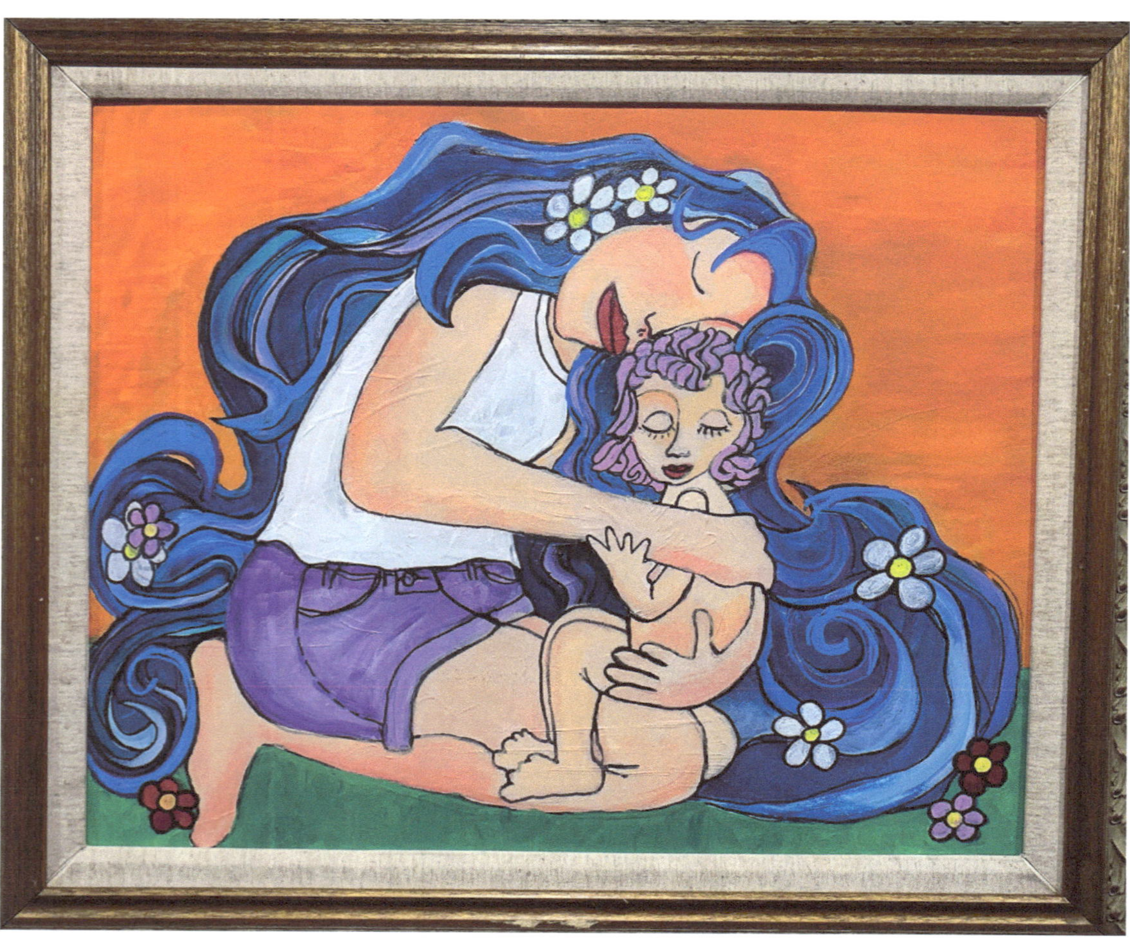

This painting was the last of my *Woman* series; yet it was truly the beginning as it came to me with a little help from my therapist who asked me a question one day (in his let's-get-right-to-the-point style). He asked me, "What do you want to be?"

I thought about it for a bit—actually, it took me a long time. Then, I looked him straight in the eye and said, "I want to be a strong, loving, courageous woman. His response was, "PROVE IT!"

I went home that day from therapy and went right to work on this painting. The strong, loving woman I was speaking of, whom I knew was very courageous in the fight of her life, was me. I realized it at that moment, right in front of me were my husband and my boys. They showed me every day that I was lovable; they kept me alive during the worst days of my life. I thought keeping my secret was keeping them protected, yet it turned out it was the other way around. They validated me and my worthiness, which I so longed for. I can see better than ever that my husband and my boys as well as my family and friends made me feel so loved. It was then I realized the woman in my painting was not my sister, but I was really painting me! It was me as I embraced my inner child. As I compassionately and lovingly held this little girl, I realized I was validating myself as a child. The child in the painting was also me. I had come full circle, and as I feverishly painted the *Strong, Loving, Courageous Woman*, I found my identity again, and I didn't need anyone else to help me validate who I had become. I knew I was ready to tell my story, my journey of finding the strong, loving, courageous woman I always was.

CHAPTER NINE

Proof I Am a Strong, Loving, Courageous Woman

When I was asked to prove why I Am a Strong, Loving, Courageous Woman…

My answer was…

…I can stand up and radically accept the journey I have been through, and to know that I still am that strong woman that is embraced by the love of my husband, children, and friends. I was given the gift that my parents believed in me, for me. Most importantly, to be able to embrace that inner child, to give myself the love and kindness I deserve. All this as I envisioned a child being embraced with the love and compassion of a strong woman, the woman that once stood as that child, who now has become her.

I took some time to find a quote that fit the strong women I have become, and I found one that seems fitting…

Life has knocked me down a few times, it showed me things I never wanted to see.
I experienced sadness and failures. But one thing for sure, I always get up.

- Alan Alexander Milne

I am continually learning that I have always been a strong woman, and my strength just shows itself in many shapes and forms. Being a strong woman means that I need to embrace and have love for myself. For way too long, I only saw myself in the twisted beliefs I created, and in what I assumed the world was saying about me…I am too big or too skinny, or too weak and scared of life. Yet I have learned that all these twisted thoughts were only my stepping stones to being a strong woman. I also realized I would continue this journey without looking for validation from others. I figured I would probably read into their words which I constantly thought were telling me to be something else. The validation has to come from myself—they have not walked my journey, or experienced what I have experienced. I need to validate myself by accepting and believing in myself. I hold dear to that embrace of the love from my father and mother who unconditionally accepted and loved me for me, and let me be me, as they did for every one of my siblings as well. Maybe the love and strength I have didn't fall far from the tree.

To be this strong, loving woman means that I recognize I am learning from the mistakes and life experiences that I have had. I can challenge my negative self-talk and learn from them. Regardless of which path I take from here, I know, more than ever, that this journey has brought me the skills I need to face new experiences. To face them with confidence, and with a willingness to participate fully, and to live life as it is a new exposure that challenges my fears, and continue to be even stronger.

To be a strong woman, I realized that the strength isn't in being like others; just simply being different makes me strong and courageous.

I am a strong woman because I'm learning that I am worthy to be respected enough to know my own limits, to set boundaries, and follow through on them. I don't need to always simply follow friends or family into things I don't agree with, or to be afraid of their rejection. I am learning to stand on my own two feet and stay true to my ideas and morals that I hold close to my heart. I can be strong as I listen to the beliefs and wisdom of others, because to be strong is to know what feels right in my heart.

To know now that I am a strong woman doesn't mean I'm not weak. It takes being a strong individual to recognize that I just may need help sometimes. Society views a strong woman as someone completely independent with no help from anyone, ever; that I would be weak if I reached out to ask for support. But truthfully, there is strength in realizing I can't do everything on my own—and it is okay to ask for help from my husband, children, friends, family, or others who have helped me to learn that all this is what keeps me strong. As one friend said, I was always strong, I just couldn't see it, but I was living it step by step.

To be a strong woman, I have to radically accept that, some days, I will look in the mirror and will have struggles to love what I see. When I do, I need to also observe my judgments and recognize them and use corrective information, which includes all the good in me as well.

I know I am strong as I recognize that, sometimes, I will not feel like a strong woman at all. I am in a trance that I feel weak, or less experienced, or less worthy, of having the word "strong" be listed in words to describe myself. I may not look like every strong woman I see around me, but that's okay—I have my own strengths, such as, I believe in others, I believe in *never say no, there is a way*. I know some experiences hurt, and some of them are my victories.

One big awareness for me as I accept and believe in myself as a strong woman is to know that on the days I struggle, I have to admit it, accept it—"it is what it is"—rather than pretending I have it all together. I need to remind myself that everyone struggles, and to pretend otherwise is just kidding myself. A strong woman doesn't always have it all together—sometimes we are still picking up the pieces off the ground and deciding where to go next. Sometimes we are still sitting in the rubble, praying that it will get easier, as we start prioritizing and take little steps out of the mess. I do know that I will eventually get back up again.

My strength is still just that—strength. And as a strong, loving woman, no matter how it may appear to others, I believe in myself, I am that strong, loving courageous woman. I want to be that all-empowering, strong, loving woman, that when my feet hit the floor each morning the devil says, "Oh crap, she's up!"

CHAPTER TEN

My Husband Unlocks His Silent Pain

The toll on the whole family: the view from my husband.

I am learning more and more how my pain and suffering was not mine alone. My eating disorder, compounded by the trauma I endured, played heavily on my whole family—my parents, siblings, husband, children, friends, and co-workers.

My Husband's view:

"It was non-stop. This disease made no sense. Her behaviors were so extreme."

As I was writing this book and sharing aspects of it with my husband, he said to me, "You should put a chapter in there about what a husband goes through when his wife is constantly battling with an eating disorder, and then, add to that her trauma. Hell, that's a book in itself."

I smirked and said, "Oh, you are lucky to have me. At least I'm not high maintenance."

"Oh," was his reaction. "You are, and have always been, more than high maintenance."

He continued, "I never knew if you were coming or going. There were times you were so frail and sick, I didn't know if I was going to come home to find you dead or alive."

So, my husband was actually voicing his feelings, which he never really does. Plus, I never realized or thought it affected him as much as he was now telling me it did. I always thought my trauma and my eating disorder were *my* pain and *my* suffering. My husband quickly pointed out that much of what I went through, he was going through as well. I was like, *What? I'm the one going through it, and what happened to me later in life, well, I would never wish it on anyone. So what was he talking about?*

I thought to myself, *he has no idea what I went through.* Then it hit me as he went on and recalled things…his memories were of my eating disorder—behaviors which I don't even recall because I was too sick to remember.

I just never looked at how much pain I put him through. Not because I didn't care, but because this eating disorder took me into what I call "my own little world." All I could handle feeling or thinking was controlling what and how, if anything, I was going to eat.

Let me share with you how many of our family members and friends saw my husband's and my relationship. Actually, I was proud everyone saw how we were a wonderful, loving, couple. We had a wonderful relationship. That was what they saw, and that too is what I believed.

So on that day when he was so frank about what he "went through," he said one phrase that hit me hard: "THERE WAS NO TRUST AND RESPECT." As I sat there taking in all he was saying, I just cried. I felt a blow to my stomach. *I love him! What is he talking about?* We have been married for 31 years. Sure, there were bumps in the road; but as he sat there recalling them, I was in shock.

I finally asked my husband, "Why did you stay?" He started with how and why he fell in love with me. He said he loved what a warm, loving person I was, and that I always was there to help or care for others. He went on to say that he knew that was always in me, it was just lost temporarily because I was struggling with the eating disorder and the trauma I went through. He went on to say, "I just had to keep this family together."

Listening to his view on everything felt like a devastating blow—my family is and always will be my priority. As I listened, I realized I was blinded by the effects of my eating disorder and what it did to my family who meant everything to me—I would never hurt them!!!

He continued, sometimes with his humor in tow. (I learned later that our humor was probably one reason we survived this terrible disease; our humor was used to mask our feelings.) It was so incredibly sad as I continued to listen to him telling me his side of the pain and suffering.

He admitted that he did notice early on in our relationships that there were some "interesting behaviors," such as my need to be on the run at all times (a behavior I still exhibit to this day). In therapy we call that my Go-Go-Go attitude, which was all about numbing out from things I couldn't handle. He reminded me that when we first met, all I ever ate was sweet potatoes and popcorn. Then he pointed out all the times I would change from one strange combination of food to another. He claims those things never really worried him back then. "Now," he said, "I realize these were only a few warning signs of a very serious eating disorder," which he said he still doesn't understand.

Then he pointed out that I seemed to get lost into such rules and behaviors which ultimately disengaged me from my family. I was blinded by this, and it was what it was because we never could talk about it, and if we tried to, I was so disconnected I would have never understood. We both hated conflict. My running full-tilt moved into my work area. I was still on the run, "but from what?" he questioned. He noted how I would work until the early mornings and that I never slept.

As our discussion continued, he said there was no time to see any warning signs. He was trying to manage his job and take care of the kids because his wife was becoming more and more consumed with her eating disorder. He claims I was in my own world, going 100 mph, unaware that I had such an obvious issue. Yes, I recall I was very strict with my diet. But I thought it wasn't a problem. I always lived with patterns, schedules, and rituals.

We had been married 31 years when I decided I was really in a great spot. I found a better understanding of what was going on and how to regulate my emotions so I wouldn't have to deal with relying on my behaviors. I wanted to write this book to help others. It's been many years, and I have never sat down like this and had a candid conversation with my husband about my eating disorder and my trauma. Sure, we had words here and there, but never a sit-down discussion.

My husband simply said, "Your eating disorder and behaviors were overwhelming." One episode he pointed out was a food pattern I was stuck in. This was so hard on him as he always tried to comply with my patterns, trying to help me. Yet later we learned he was enabling me. He was just trying to help and take care of the family. He said he was very aware how rigid my food pattern had become, and that my world would crumble if I couldn't stick to my rules and patterns I was developing. This occurred as my OCD (obsessive-compulsive disorder) was growing as I got sicker and the stronger food patterns developed.

As I was writing this book, and had this conversations with my husband. I was devastated when he said it affected our **trust and respect**. What the heck did he mean? I didn't ask for this eating disorder, and I certainly didn't ask for my life to come crashing down on me as I was traumatically assaulted and raped, which left me hospitalized in a fetal position. How could he say that!??!

As he continued to speak, I was starting to recall and accept that he was right; I was so sick that I was acting against my values and morals. I really was manipulating him in so many ways just to allow me to keep my eating disorder a secret. I recalled how I would ask him, "Please fill my car with gas, because I have no time in the morning before work." But my ulterior motive was to send him away so I could purge my dinner. *Me, deceitful? I loved him and my children. I would never do anything to hurt them.* These are the thoughts that went through my head.

As I stood back and recalled even more of the pain I put my husband and children through, more tears ran down my face. I recalled the time when I lay in the hospital for 30 days in a coma. I never looked at it from his point of view—I was the one in the coma (and this happened more than once). But when I saw it from their viewpoint, it broke my heart. My husband talked about himself and my children sitting almost daily, 30 days of my being in a coma, and watching their mother lifeless with tubes coming out of her everywhere; the phone calls he received while at work, from the doctors requesting permission to place a trach in my throat to keep me breathing.

I finally could see why he was angry sometimes. My husband is the most loving person I know. He would do anything for friends and family, especially his wife and children.

When he said it felt as if I didn't care about how it affected him or our children, it broke my heart again, because I knew that my husband and children kept me alive this whole time. I just couldn't see how far the disease took me away from them. How could I have done this? They are and always have been the loves of my life.

I always thought, *what was wrong, what was missing?* I didn't realize at the time that the pain and suffering I was going through was destroying the most important part of my life. My husband also noted how he never knew the whole affect it had on me too because of my secrets and lies, and how I kept my experience to myself.

My husband pointed out how he didn't understand my bizarre rituals and fears around food. He also pointed out he didn't understand why I couldn't just get over what happened to me, as years kept going by and I stayed stuck. He said it broke his heart as he watched me slowly self-destruct, right before his own eyes. He said it just made no sense at the time. Why couldn't I just move on? Then he used the words that we drilled into our kids as they were growing up: the importance of Trust and Respect. It was so painful to hear him say that my eating disorder took away what I truly believed in, and that he felt there was no trust or respect between us. I didn't realize how destructive my eating disorder was, and early on I was blinded to anything he was saying. Hell, I didn't even know I really *had* an eating disorder at one point.

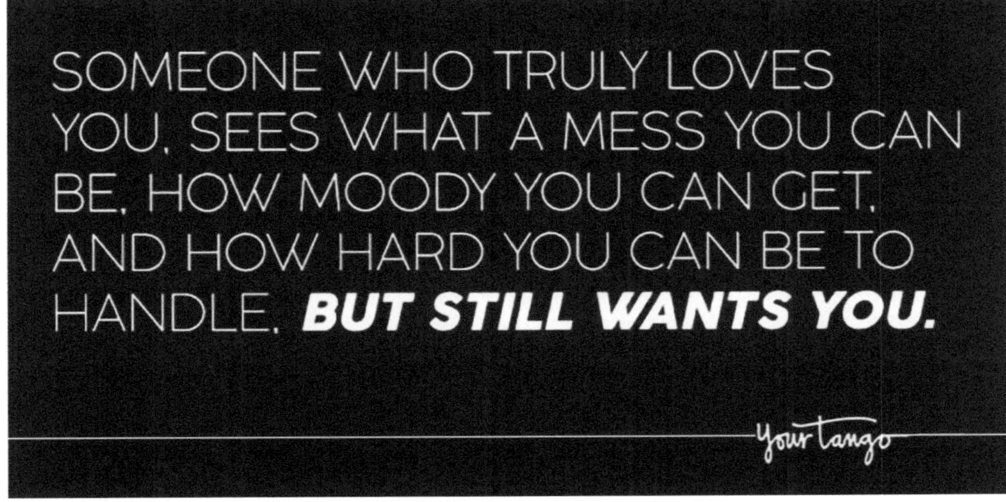

My husband then said softly, "I felt I was alone, confused, betrayed…as my own wife was destroying not only herself, but our relationship, and our family. I didn't know how to fix it. At one point, at the height of her eating disorder, I came to the conclusion that, *I was done, I would divorce her and her own demise.*"

He continued, "It was much later that we then added the effects of the trauma, which was also confusing. It was her secret for so long. Then, when the truth came out, I still didn't see why she just couldn't move on, and I thought things were bad before, now I was faced many times over with the fact she might die. I saw the fear in my children's eyes when she was in the comas and nearly died. Why? Because of an eating disorder? Still, this made no sense, and I resented her for all she put us through.

"Now, I am so proud and happy we learned and grew together through this disease and the toll of the trauma. I'm glad I didn't leave when things got really tough. I knew I had to stay to keep our family together. It was not her journey alone. It was *our* journey to love and respect each other, which also added to her self-love."

Looking back on our journey of healing, we found this quote, which represents the continuous growth of our love.

"I'd rather have bad times with you, than good times with someone else.
I'd rather be beside you in a storm, than safe and warm by myself.
I'd rather have hard times together, than to have it easy apart.
I'd rather have the one who holds my heart."

\- Unknown

CHAPTER ELEVEN

Final Thoughts

What I want from my book is to provide all the energy and passion that went into writing it, to be put to use for others. This is for individuals who are dealing with some form of trauma, eating disorder, or who need a hand to get through some mental health issue. This book is designed to tell my story of what I experienced and how the strength of my family and how my therapists helped me utilize Art Therapy as a tool along with using the DBT skills as a tool. Together these two modalities were the tools that provided a path for me to succeed and to become healthy again. I want that for everyone as their adventure to self-love while on their own journeys. My ultimate dream is to help others. I wanted this book to inspire others to believe life is worth living.

The purpose of my sharing this book came to me when I began to incorporate DBT skills with my process of using Art Therapy. This is when I realized I was beginning to understand and grow through the process. Art Therapy helped me break down what I was learning through Dialectical Behavior Therapy (DBT) skills. Along with that, I was challenged by my therapist when he asked what I wanted to be, and I answered, "A strong, loving, courageous woman." That was a huge moment for me. It separated me from my eating disorder, and it was the exact moment I decided to start this book

The two components of Art Therapy and DBT are how I found my journey. I learned that the two modalities work hand-in-hand with each other. Art Therapy helped me put the pieces of the skills together and incorporate them into my life. I was so excited and thankful about my therapist teaching me about DBT skills.

Through my journey I found that I *am* a strong, loving, courageous woman. I don't need to keep secrets—I can tell my story. I am a wife, a daughter, a mother, a sister, a friend. I am a person who enjoys reaching out and helping others. I'm creative, and I live my life by my heart. One of my strongest values is family. This book is about who I am as a person—not my past experience.

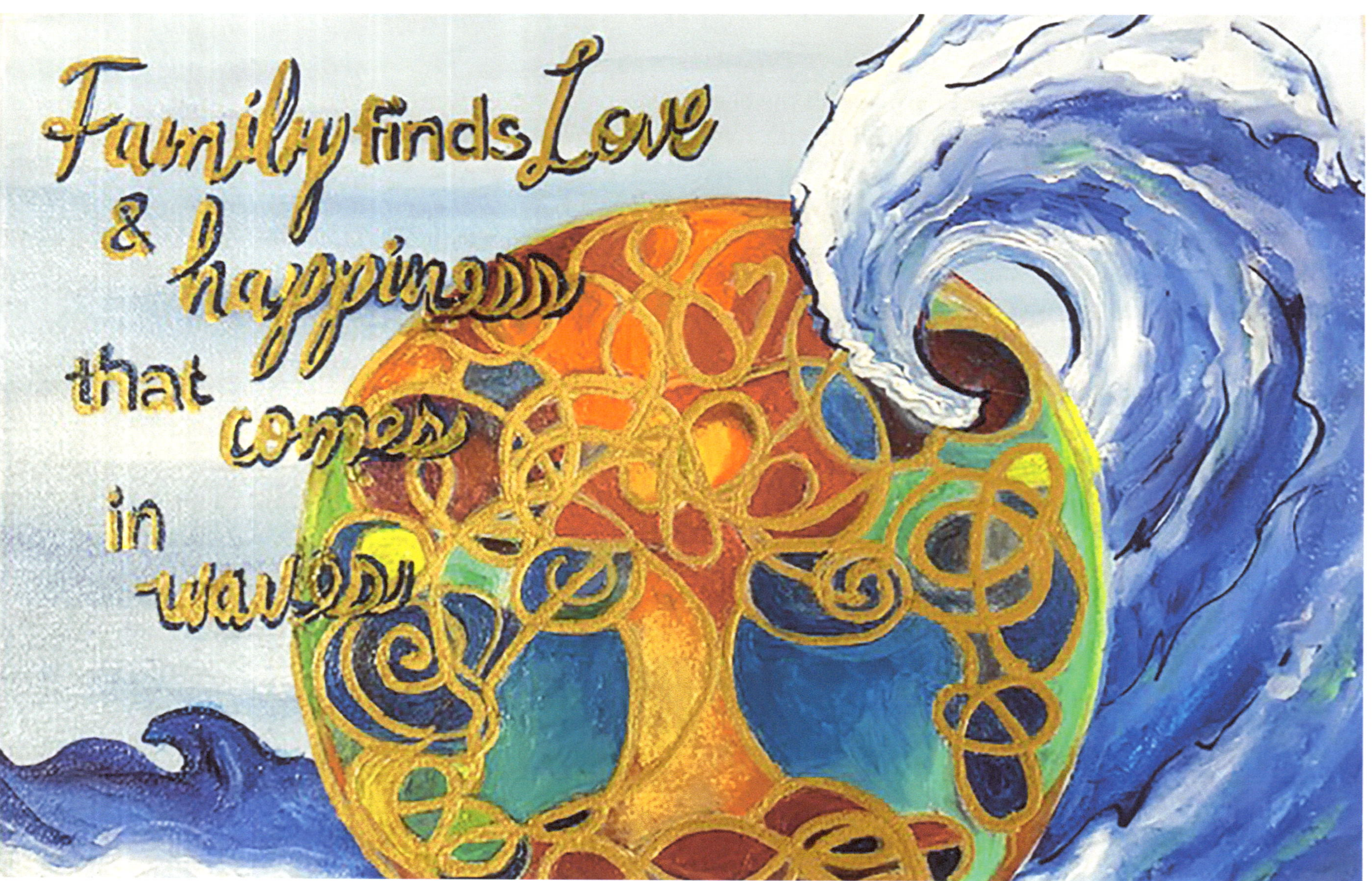
Family finds Love
& happiness
that comes
in waves

This painting represents my core value, which is my family. My family brings me happiness, and they have always been there for me. It is also true that the happiness and lessons from our families come in waves. We ride this wave because we learn from our families, teach our families, and receive support and love from one another. The wave of life may be unknown to us, but we trust our families. We can trust that as we ride the wave we experience life, because it, too, offers us the unknown. We take that ride for the experience, and to radically accept that life in the present moment becomes the experience it offers us.

The DBT skills taught me to stop and realize that everyone in my family has experienced many things. Knowing this helped me understand that everyone has different values, and we may not always see eye-to-eye, but they were my core. Sometimes we have to ride the wave, accept that it is what it is, deal with the stress, and learn from experience. For me, that is knowing that I always have my family. I love my husband and my boys more than anything and that never faltered. Family includes my siblings, extended family, and friends…they all mean so much to me.

Learning and accepting all that my family brings to me helped me get through my life of anxiety and fear. My eating disorder put blinders on me. I missed opportunities to experience all the love of my family because I was so busy believing I had to prove to everyone I was worthy and that I had to win their approval. I was constantly trying to show them my love for them.

Family Values/Riding the Wave is of the family tree, and of a wave that represents that sometimes we may be faced with life's struggles, but if we ride the wave, it will set us free. As I took off my blinders and made the changes I needed to make, I was able to radically accept that I was riding the wave.

Utilizing the skills, the wave has calmed to the point that I can see the beauty of the legacy that my parents left, which was the importance of family. It is so worth riding the wave, taking the journey, learning self-love, and finally opening my eyes to all the love around me which gave me the strength to heal.

This newfound growth provided me the time and happiness with my husband and my boys, who grew up watching me struggle physically and mentally. But now I have my whole life to live with them in a much healthier way. I want for all the readers to see and understand that my journey was unique for me; we all have our own experiences. Telling you about finding the right tools (like for me finding both the Art Therapy and DBT skills), along with asking for help, was my way of sharing how I was knocking down the boulders that I had to get through—the boulders that blocked my way to a healthy life. But now I can share these experiences with my family, my boys, and now with you, the reader, who hopefully can use the boulders you knock down as your steppingstones to explore your own experiences, your own journey, and the paths that you must take to enrich your life and your family's life, so you can be whole again.

Remember, the main goal of DBT is to balance two opposites that are constantly existing: acceptance and change. This balance enhances the quality of healing, and anyone using DBT will be constantly learning and working towards this balance. This balance will help a person change the negative behaviors.

I believe that Art Therapy for both adults and children who have experienced trauma becomes a tool that offers the individuals a way to express themselves freely. The power of art and art making helped me to get through the memories and become aware of my emotions and how the emotions functioned for me before, during, and after my trauma. As a survivor of abuse, and being an Art Therapist myself, I found that the creative process was a safe way for me to communicate and work with my therapist who could help me get in touch with the traumatic memories. My therapeutic process utilized both the art making and processing of my art, alongside my learning the skills of DBT. My creative outlet was my visual art, but creativity shines in many ways. For example, poetry, writing, music, acting…the list goes on. What I'm trying to say is that my creative outlet helped me channel my feelings, express myself, learn new ways to look at problematic behaviors, and to assist in the understanding of my new DBT skills. Both the art and DBT helped me to find my voice and my words. This provided me a way to get in touch with myself so I could tell my story and heal. I had a mantra that I stated earlier, it was something that I came up with at a very young age, it says, *never say no—there is a way*. Well, with this experience, I believe that to be true; for me, it was the process of utilizing Art Therapy and connecting it to DBT skills which brought me the success I needed to get through these traumatic memories. I am back in the driver's seat living my life.

Most importantly, I learned that I can continue to use my Art Therapy and the DBT skills to carry on with a healthy life, even to my everyday adventures. This allows me the most important thing in my life, and that is the value of family.

The strongest person who stood beside me, protected me, and provided me a safe environment was my husband. My husband always was there for me. I close with this picture that he took in North Dakota, a place where he would always take me and our boys. North Dakota brings me, my husband, and our family memories, freedom, the joy of visiting the families we spend time with, and time with Mother Nature and all that God has provided us. My first few trips to North Dakota were meeting the families we stayed with. Those families represented the sheer beauty of what family stands for.

I witnessed hard-working individuals and their genuineness as they opened their homes and hearts to us. They truly enjoyed sharing the ins and outs of farm life. The backbone to all their success and happiness is their everlasting bond of love, faith, and strength their families stand for.

When I stood in those fields, I could see all that beauty for miles and miles all around me. I realized how small I am in comparison to the world around me, and it made me think that all my worries and traumatic experiences are so small in perspective as I work through my journey. That was a big moment for me. It completely changed my outlook on my life.

Life is a journey, and it's about growing and changing and coming to terms with who and what you are, and loving who and what you are.

It is important to remember that everyone has their own unique journey, and we all may need a little help finding our voice. I believe when you're ready to work on your journey there are many avenues to take which will help guide you through self-healing. It was natural for me to use Art Therapy combined with the exciting new skills of DBT. It is a lot of work, but every step of the way is rewarding.

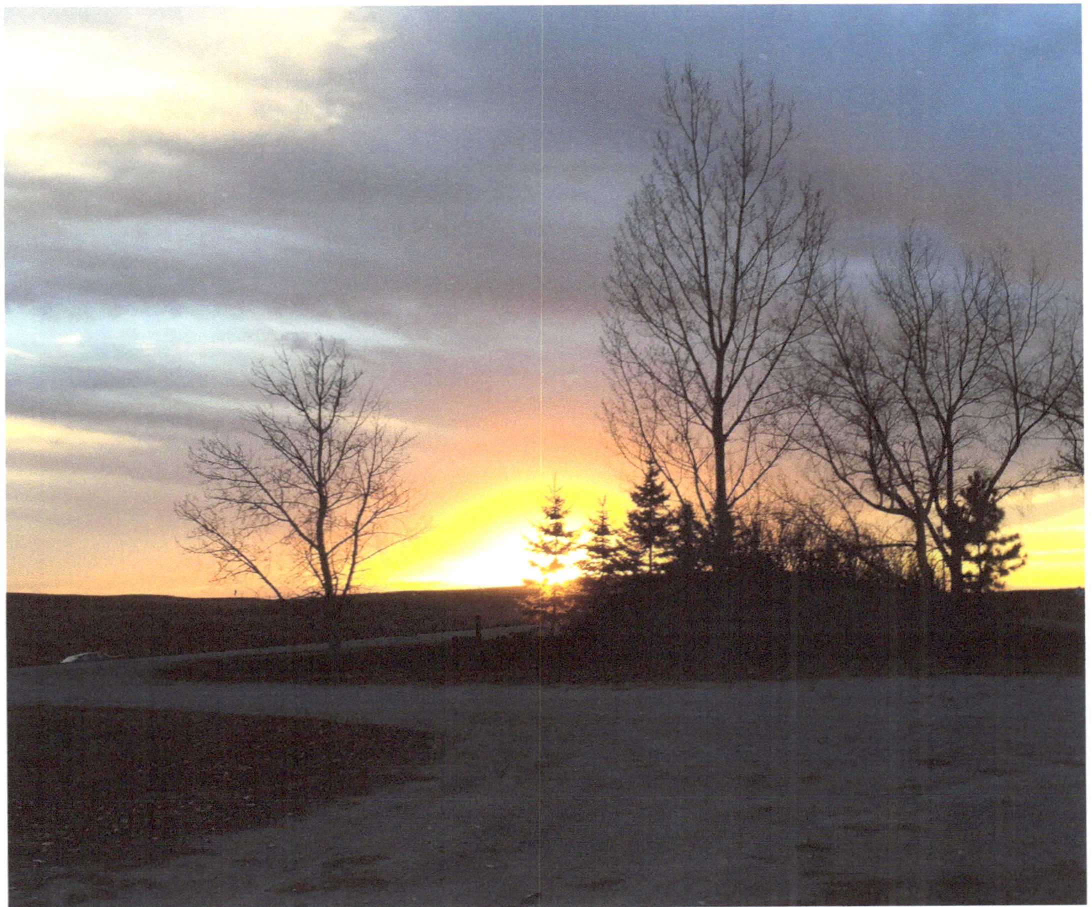

Giving an opportunity for a young artist to grow:

This is for you, M.P.

This is dedicated to one of the many artists who I worked with over the years. Art Therapy and providing opportunities for my students to succeed are a few of my passions. One day the two crossed paths. I have a client who wants to be a successful writer. I was wowed when I read the work of this young writer. I could see that she caught every detail needed for a story, with subtle changes that catch the reader's attention. I wanted to give her the opportunity to share her gift. Along with this opportunity, I presented her a challenge: write a poem or a story and then I would meet it with a drawing. In return, she had to pick one of my art pieces and write about it.

I present to you one of her poems she shared with me. Below the poem is our artwork which we did as we processed the meaning of her poem and our feelings.

The second part of the challenge was to write about my artwork. She chose *Loss* and *dance of two*.

Poem : **"In love"**

By MP

Based on the painting *In Love*
by Kathleen Kaufman

in love

They say it like it's a place
 a place you can feel
 a place you can see
 a place you can exist in

 I do not know what it is like to say those words
To feel that place
to see that place
 to exist in that place

do the syllables curl around your lips
what does it feel like
what does it look like
 what is it

I wish to know
what it feels like
 what it looks like
 what it is like to exist in that place

 someone take me there
please

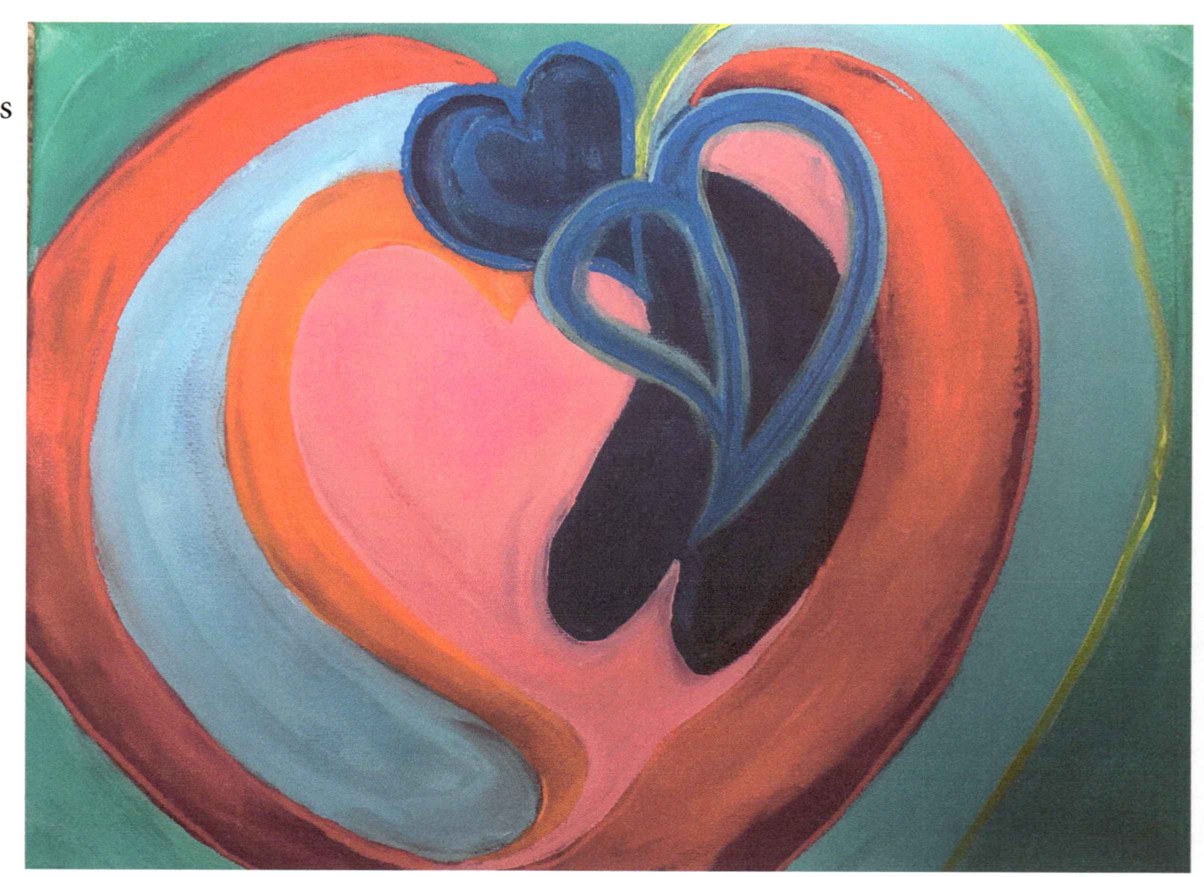

"Basic Parts"

by M.P.

Based on the paintings *Loss* and *dance of two*
by Kathleen Kaufman

"Life is unmanageable."

"Life is painful."

"Life is uncontrollable."

"Lies," I say.

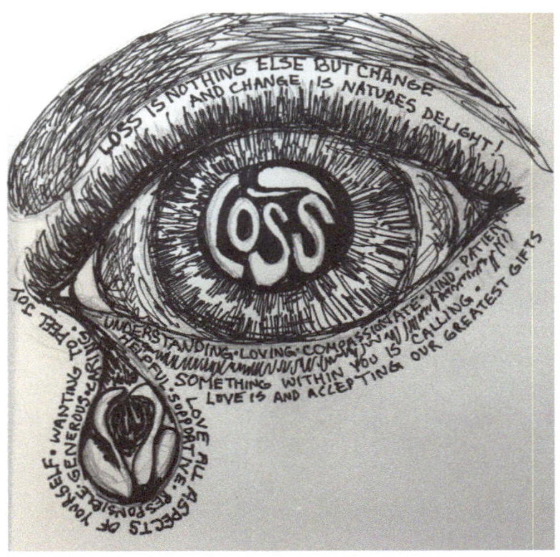

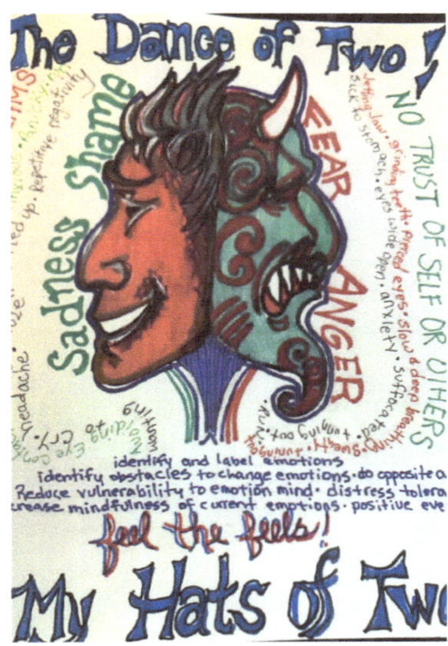

Over time, these statements are shoved down our throats as if, without these facts, we wouldn't be able to digest the horrors of our world. Albeit subtle, they are ingrained nonetheless. Even if, by some miracle, nobody required this information to be a staple of your conscious mind, you've probably discovered it all on your own.

Do not believe the words of the evil one.

He would rather you believe this world is unlivable than to see you blossom and share your life with the rest of the world. He'd rob you of your oxygen before he would let you thrive. He whispers in your delicate ear, "You're all alone. You can't cure it. You lost. Nobody's here. Just you, me, and the sweet release of…"

To that, I say, "Loss is nothing more than change and change is nature's delight!"

To that, I say, "No matter if you win or lose, the most important thing in life is to enjoy what you have!"

At the end of the day, what do we *really* have? When we are broken down into our basic parts, what do you find? A tsunami of tears ready to burst the dam behind our eyes? A noose around our neck, choking out what people want to hear? A powerless sack of skin and organs that is crashing against the rapids of time? What about secrets even the Lord would shudder to hear? A heart of stone and soul of thorns?

NO.

When we are broken down into our basic parts, there are emotions that are raw and real. There is endless potential in every living being on Earth; even if they are blind, deaf, or cut off from the truth, it is still there. There are eyes that see the cracks in the past, glue in the present, and faith in the future. Broken down into our basic parts, there is anguish, joy, fear, hopelessness, and there is love—love that heals, love that frees, and love that has no boundaries.

The evil one puts the lies of this world into our heads so we will ignore our capacity to love, our capacity to fix, our capacity to discover. In our ignorance, we give in to his deceptions, his lies.

His hate.

Look in the mirror. Truly look.

You will see him, standing there with his bony fingers gripping your shoulder as the whispers continue; "Give up. It's useless. Come with me. I can help it end—"

When you see his cold, gut-wrenching hands around you, run!

You run until the breath that fills your lungs raises you into the air. You run until your light blinds him. You run until you can look back at him as he dissolves into ashes. You run until you make it to the end of his dark tunnel. You run until you realize who was truly powerless all along.

Him.

He is desperate for your attention, your care, your *love* because he has none of his own. He feeds off the time and energy you spend with him and he will not stop until you make the choice to stand and run away. He will not stop until you put him in his place. He will not stop until you prove that you are stronger than the lies he implants in your mind.

When broken down into our basic parts, we are fragile, fearful, and more powerful than we will ever know because we have someone he never will: God.

The lesson was we all have our life's experiences, and with these life experiences we may see things in a different way. We may have different viewpoints because of these experiences. So instead of judging someone or arguing with them, maybe we should just see them as someone with a different viewpoint, as someone who sees things differently, and maybe you can see them in a positive, constructive way.

I thank her dearly and look forward to her success as a writer.

Afterword

With all of the preceding information about DBT, learning about the skills, and how to build mastery of these skills, my journey to keep learning about these skills and to keep incorporating them into my everyday life will continue.

I've always wanted to write a book about the details of my eating disorder or the details of my trauma—not a "tell all"—but a book that helps individuals find their journey to health. I felt that this book was an opportunity to show how I learned to share my story. I was a registered Art Therapist working hard to help individuals with disabilities find ways to adapt and succeed by using Art Therapy. I also worked with children who were chronically ill; they, too, benefitted by using Art Therapy. My passions were art and helping individuals succeed. My all-time mantra was *never say no—there is a way*, meaning: with art as our tool, we can find ways to succeed in life. It was then I realized that my art had told my story all along; it was just without using words at first. I used my art as the impetus to tell my story, and it was my way to reach out. I found that art became my voice. As I continued to draw, I was also being taught DBT skills. With my newfound tools to help me be assertive and ask for what I needed, I began the journey to healing. The most intriguing piece was learning that my passion for Art Therapy went hand-in-hand with my learning and understanding of DBT skills. The art I was expressing was helping me to grasp how to comprehend the DBT skills and incorporate them into my life. So I learned quickly, that while experiencing the indignity of being helpless and at the mercy of another person, I now was given the opportunity to express the feeling of being powerless and trapped in my own body.

As I was about to finish this chapter, I realized I had these additional pieces of artwork and sketches from my journals that I had done over the years. This art really captured a timeline of where I was and how far I've come.

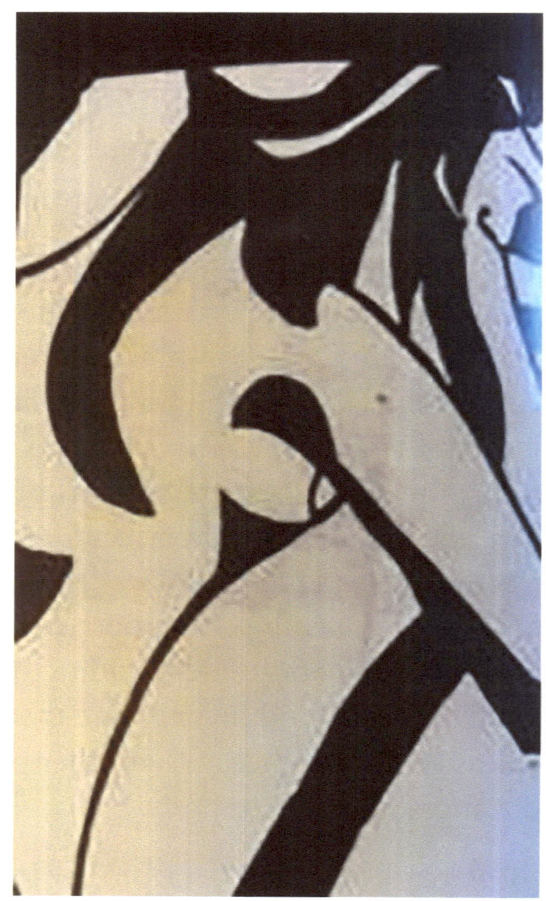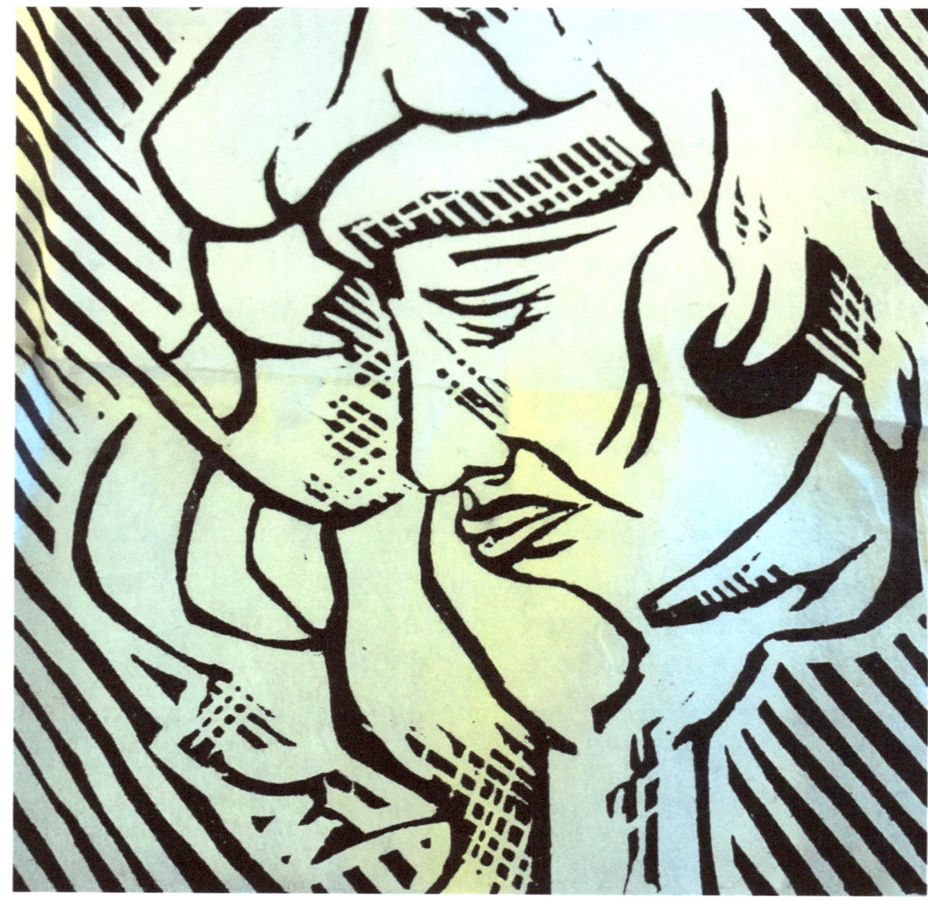

These prints represent images I had while my negative thinking ran wild. Generally, whenever there was stress in my life, I turned to all the negative thinking I had stored in my head. My automatic thoughts were that I was fat, ugly, and disgusting. During this time in my life, I was searching for my lost identity, which many of my paintings actually focused on. These are monoprints during a time I had nothing but black-and-white thinking. I saw myself as a defective person, and that I must be a bad person because of what happened. It was like my eating disorder battled in my head; constantly at war with myself and my negative talk.

The following clay sculptures of the two heads were made earlier in my life. These eyeless sculptures were my way of saying I didn't know who I was as a person. I had no identity because the eating disorder stole that from me. As time went on, my eating disorder took complete control of me. My identity was just that, eyeless and numb to my own life experiences.

More recently I created another clay head, but to my surprise, this one included eyes. It definitely had more life and a strong personality. Again, it was as if my art was tuned in to my own growth and healing. The sculpture's eyes were wide open to who I was—not numb, but full of life.

I have come far in my journey. I see this as an additional step in my life's timeline and how my art continues to document each step I've made toward self-acceptance. This also shows that my eyes are wide open to something that Neal taught me: to say no, to stop raising my hand to volunteer for things, and then to delegate. My newfound skills were helping me to be more assertive so I could ask for what I needed and I could take another step in my journey of healing.

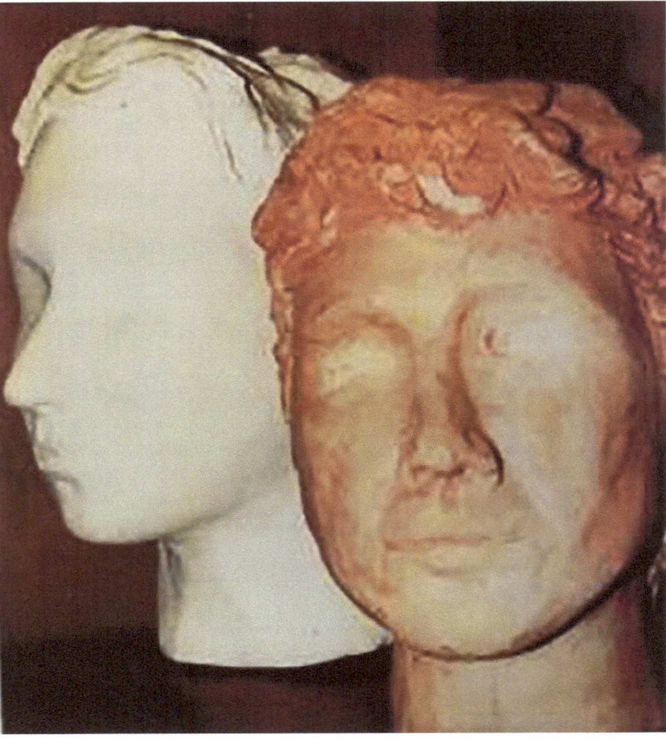

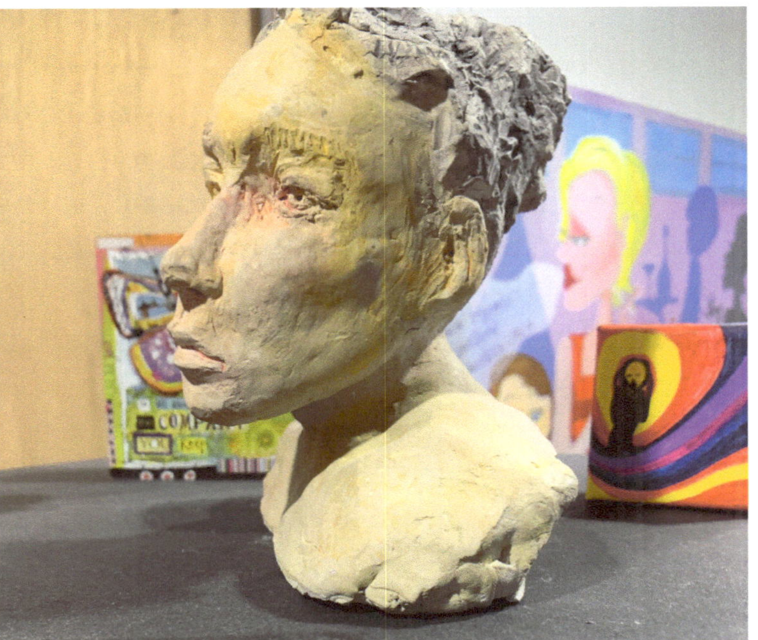

I was learning how my past and present artwork was helping me to achieve a better understanding of what I was being taught. Often Dr. Laura and I would sit and process my artwork during our sessions. This truly helped me to see how much of my life was ruled by my past life experiences and how the eating disorder took the reins and ran with my life. Dr. Laura and I could see the development and my growth as I was incorporating these new skills into my life. This joint work solidified the growth I was making in my life, and my understanding of how to connect it all together was portrayed in my art. Using my art and the process of Art Therapy combined with DBT skills marked my journey. I could have added tears of happiness to the sculpture because I now know I have the strength, plus the skills I need to keep growing in making real gains in this journey of life.

As I began this journey, I scurried around looking at my old sketches that I've kept for years. These journals and sketchbooks remind me of where I was and how I learned to say the things in my head about myself. I was learning that these were judgments which continually belittled me and beat me down—I didn't realize at the time that I was constantly judging myself. Later I realized that's what kept me stuck in suffering. These negative and judgmental thoughts were automatic and constant. It is hard to believe how much I would beat myself up with these negative thoughts, and how I captured this pain in so many of my old sketches.

I feel it is worth repeating that my art and DBT showed my growth as I began to challenge these judgmental thoughts using facts. I found that when I was deep into my eating disorder (which, as I reminded myself, was a very unhealthy coping mechanism), I used it as my coping skill for the most difficult experiences in my life, especially the trauma. I can look at these journals and realize I was probably trying to find the words I so longed for to get the help I needed. My thoughts were like a broken record; there was validity to them. My art captured my pain; it was the only way I knew how to communicate. I then began focusing on the true values in my life and my personal beliefs of who I really was and what I stood for. I needed to step away from my judgmental thoughts that I created, that continued to grow as my eating disorder took over. I was told to make a list of who I was, and my list was that I was a loving, caring, genuine person, whose goal in life was to help individuals with special needs. So each day I needed to be mindful of what I was thinking and feeling in the moment, and to be aware of my judgmental thinking, and, use my wise mind. It was my choice to do what was effective to accomplish my goal of a life worth living. This is just the kind of thinking that I needed to help me get out of the black hole.

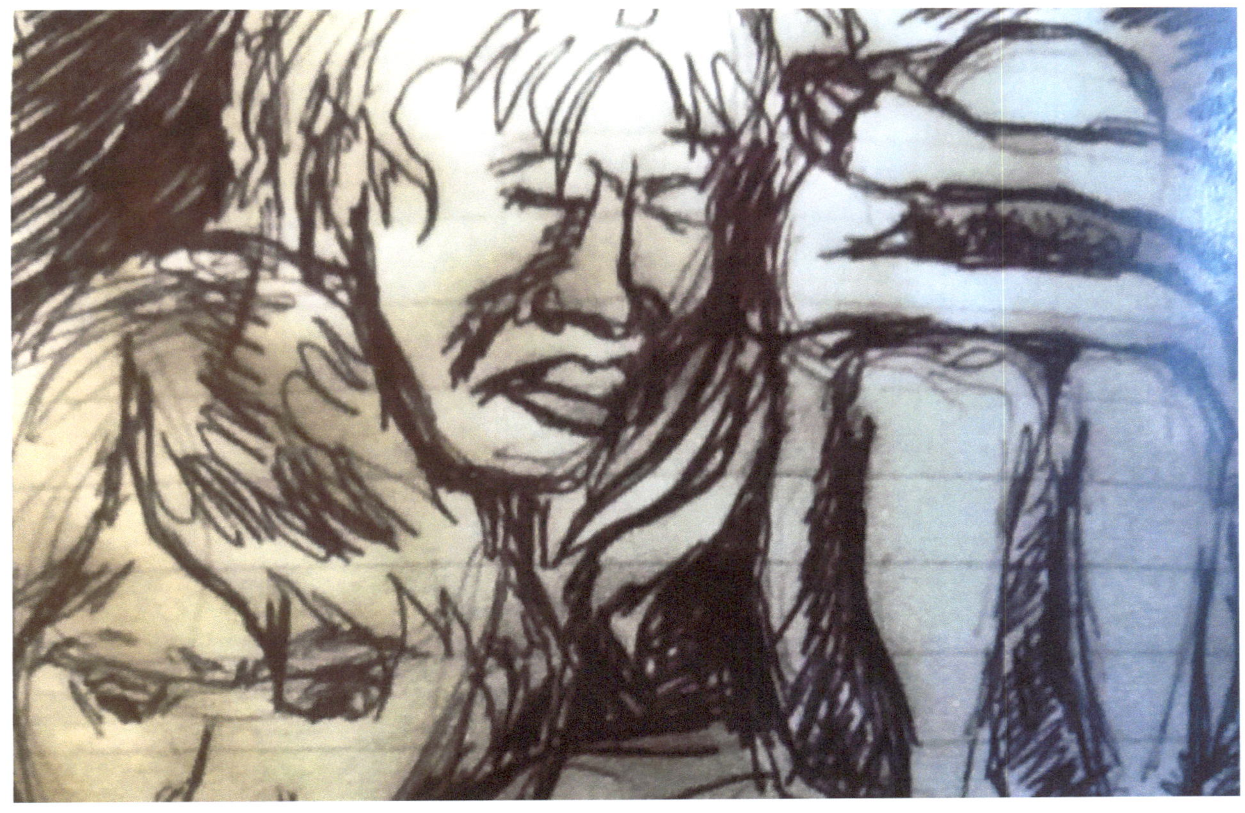

Art came naturally to me, but anyone can come forward and use Art Therapy as I did. Art Therapy has become so helpful for me to break the barriers from my trauma. It helped me to experience and explore my memories in a safe way. Art Therapy opened the doors for me to express my internal experience.

I return to my painting, *Turning the Mind*. This painting represents the DBT skill of the same name. The painting and skill are ultimately choosing the path—the path that gives you a chance to make changes in your life for the better. Trust me, you might have to use this skill over and over and over again as you encounter the need to redirect yourself back on your path to a life worth living.

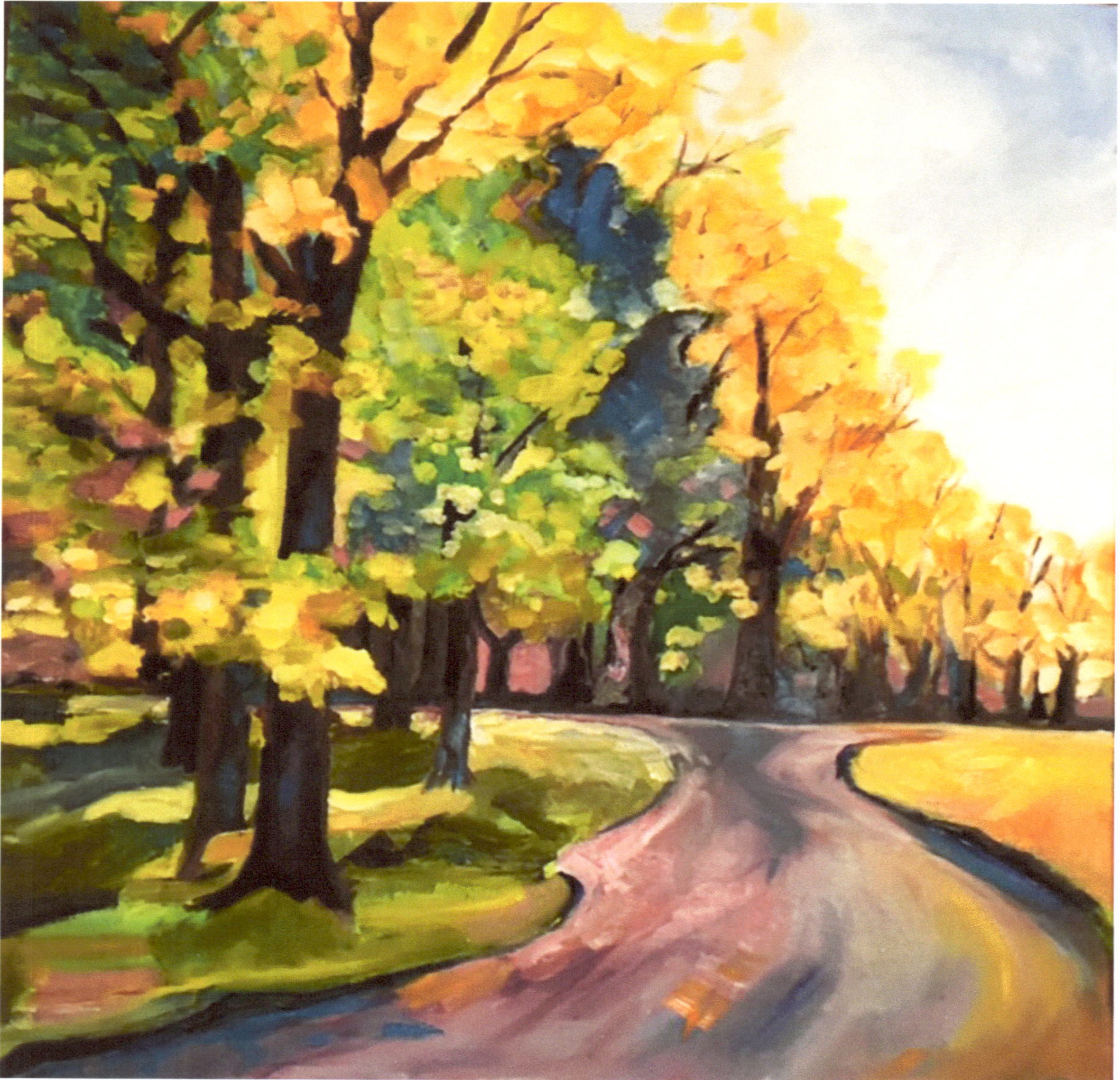

Turning the Mind

Along the way of my journey, I created numerous sketches. That was my only tool I was able to use to try to reach out and tell my story. My story and my experience were my secret, yet I so much wanted to say the words. The words were locked in me as my experience was truly my fear. Art had become my voice, and I was also beginning to understand and use the DBT skills.

The next picture, *Fear and Anger*, is supposed to help show all the fear and anger I had stirred up in me. But looking closer, just as in *Loss*, there is corrective information written on the hands and arms, showing my understanding that in those scary hands, the corrective information wasn't actually as scary as I thought. Instead of saying, *Why did this happen to me*? I said, *I am a survivor—a victim I am NOT!* and, *Don't judge yourself by what others did to you.*

The most intriguing piece was learning that my passion of Art Therapy went hand-in-hand with learning and understanding DBT skills. Using my art was helping me to grasp how to comprehend the DBT skills and how I could incorporate them into my life. So I learned quickly that I was able to validate my experience that had brought me nothing but the feelings of indignity and helplessness at the hands of another person. I realized then that my art was giving me the opportunity to express feelings of fear and anger; fear of being powerless and trapped in my own body, and finding the new skill—corrective information, which is now incorporated into my life—so I could heal.

Fear and Anger

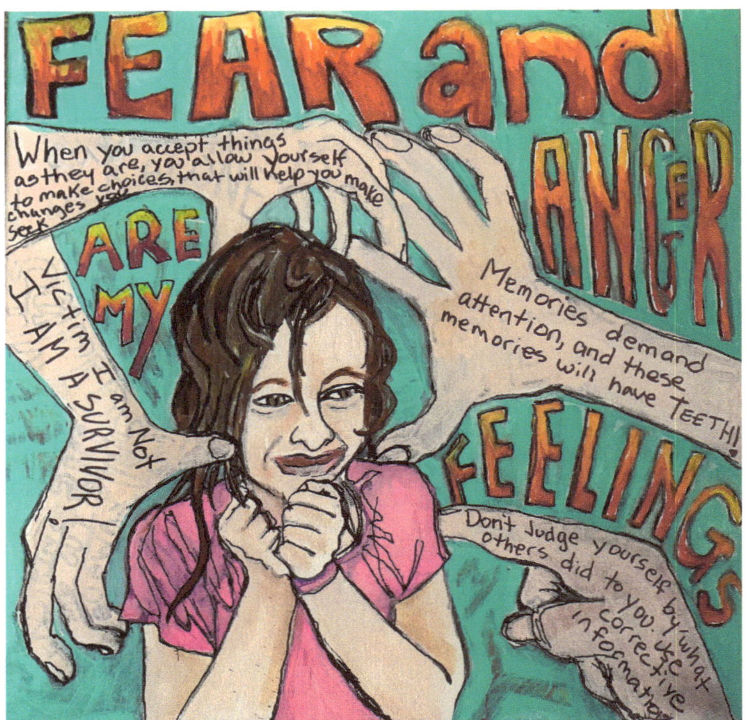

I saw these pieces of artwork which I did along my journey. Looking back at all my artwork, I can see I was trying to pull all the puzzle pieces together and use my art to work through problem-solving. This sketch, done with markers, was me working through my thoughts and feelings, learning to trust, and learning how I could accept my experience and begin to enjoy the journey of self-love—all as I was learning to let go.

This was how I lived my life for a very, *very* long time. I feared that I wasn't good enough and that I was defective. I always had this belief, even as a child. My traumatic experience and my already poor coping mechanism—my long time relationship with my eating disorder—were compounded by the fear and anger that was in me. I feared I wasn't lovable. I was also learning that, to my surprise, I actually had anger within me. I remember sitting with Dr. Laura, swearing up and down that I never had an ounce of anger in me. As a matter of fact, I didn't have *any* emotions, I was numb to *everything*. My paintings were full of my feelings; I just wasn't in touch with them. My paintings were expressing everything, and thankfully, Laura could help me look deep into the paintings and see what I was trying to say without words. The paintings helped me get in touch with my feelings. I spent most of my adult life being numb and not in touch with my feelings. Laura said to me and my publisher, when I began to write this book, that when I came into her office for the first time, I was what she called "the walking head." My head was in one place, and my body was in another. The head and body had no connection in between. I never saw that part of me because I was unaware and very numb to life. I was most likely in this state from the lack of nutrition and the lack of some basic developmental skills, and struggling with PTSD. This lack of self-awareness and the need for radical acceptance of the trauma I had gone through was so important to my journey. So this picture may *say* "Fear" and "Anger," but if you look at the arms coming to get me, on each arm is written at least one of the DBT skills which I am learning.

I am continuing to correct the negative beliefs I have of myself; I now realize I have carried them around for way too long. These beliefs were so automatic that I had to use the corrective information skill and "check the facts" over and over until I broke through my thick skull that, *yes, I am worthy and I am safe*. This is also when I realized I didn't need to search for validation from others, but just needed to believe in myself and to give myself the validation I always searched for. I'm the holder of the keys to self-validation. I had to choose the path which was of *my* values and *my* morals. I felt this came easy for me—I always lived my life by my heart and to help others. I also had to learn that, even though I may live by my heart and help others, I also need to respect my limits and boundaries and to learn not to feel guilty for taking care of myself, too. These concepts were difficult for me to radically accept.

Every day from here on out I will capitalize on all that I have learned. I take this information and sit back and grasp the moment I now cherish with a gentle heart. There is nothing stopping me on this journey because the tears in my eyes and lump in my throat are telling me these are the real feelings. I may have suffered, but now my experiences are based on the God-given moments and memories I have, and the new memories I will cherish with my family. My silver lining is that, on this journey, I gained knowledge of my own self-love; and that, with this love, I found more room in my heart to cherish the time with my family…that special time is to be with my husband and kids, to love them and be loved more than anything.

Now I never want to put my paint brush down—I have so much more to say! I can see how working on an art piece helped me solidify a particular skill, and how I was interpreting it and could incorporate it into my life. I truly recommend to anyone who is getting in touch with their feelings to just start putting down thoughts and feelings on paper or canvas—anything from a doodle, to a piece of artwork, or even a story, a poem, or a play. I believe this will help you let your true feelings out.

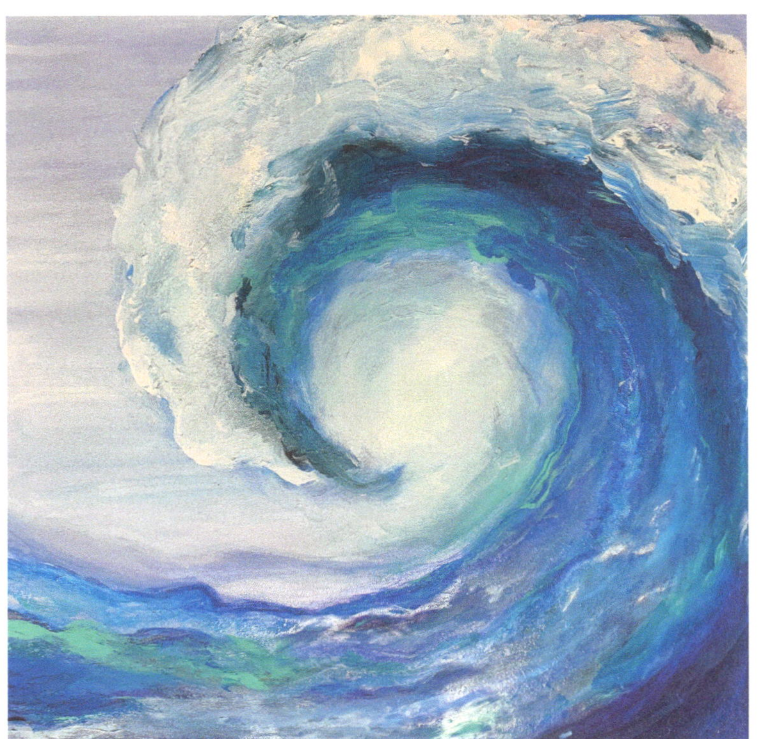

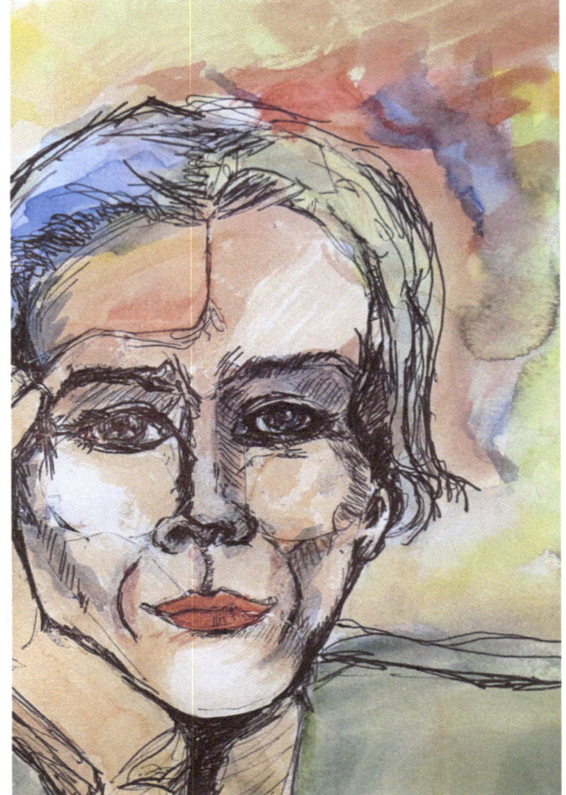

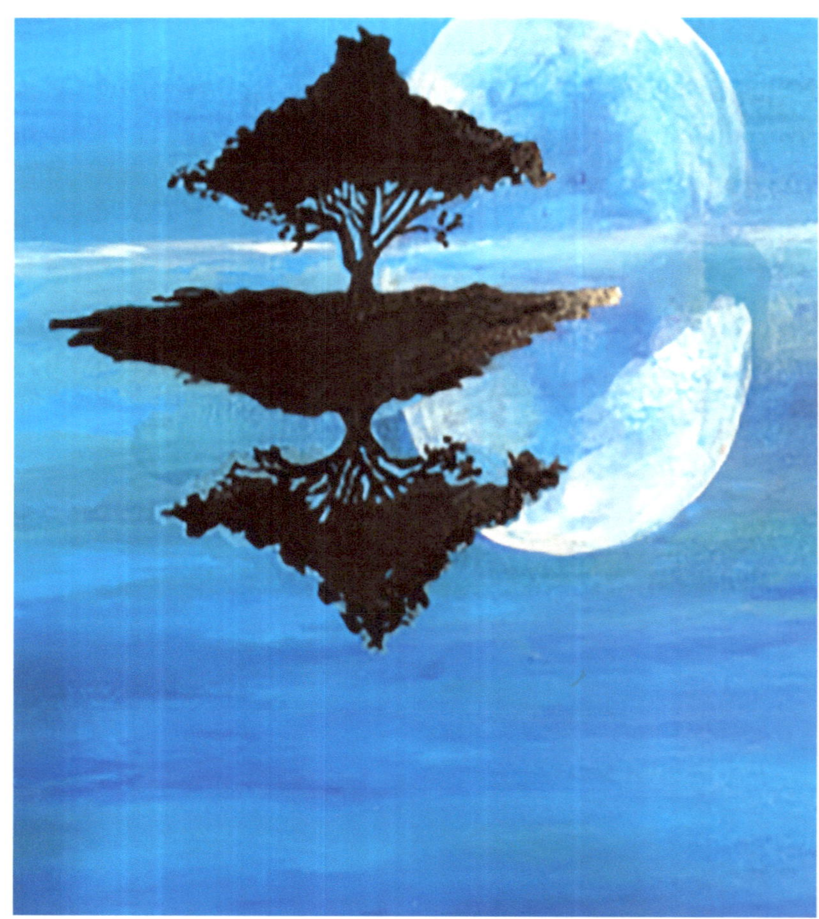

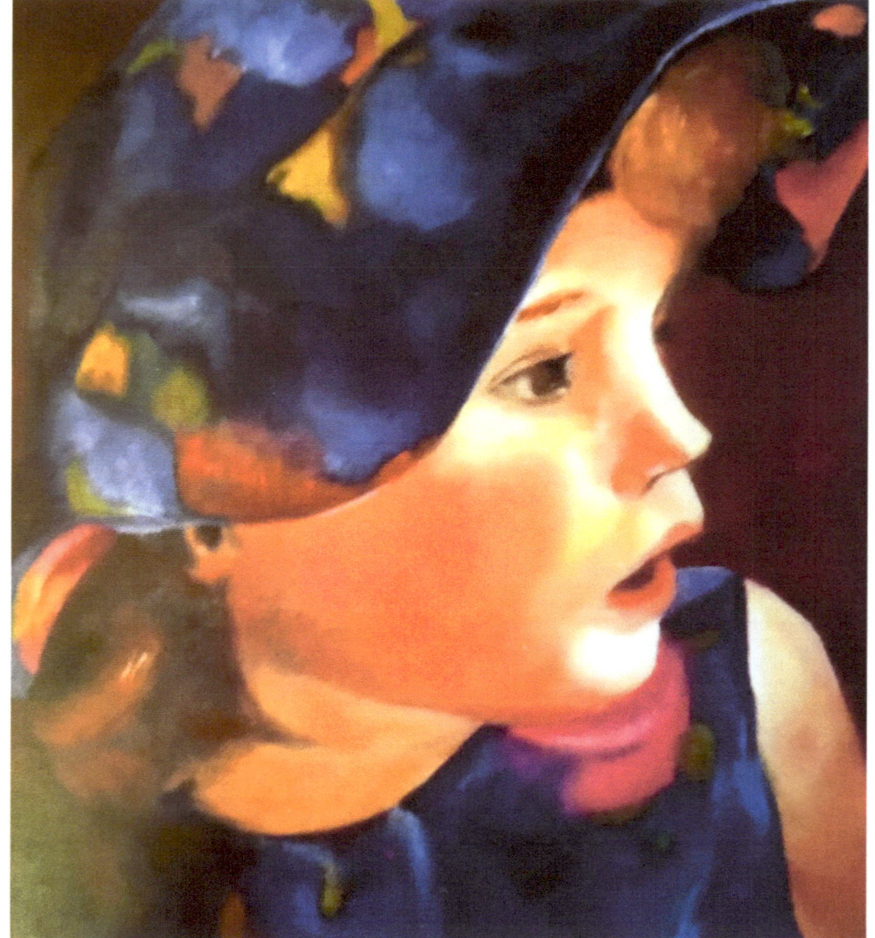

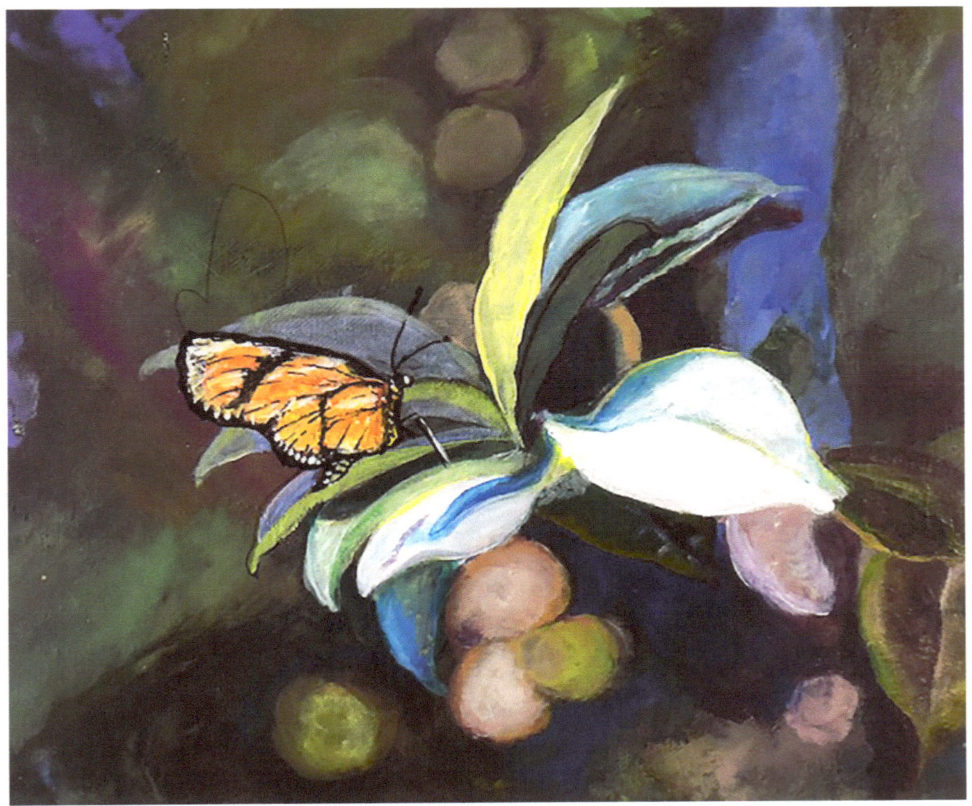

Here's to You, Mom

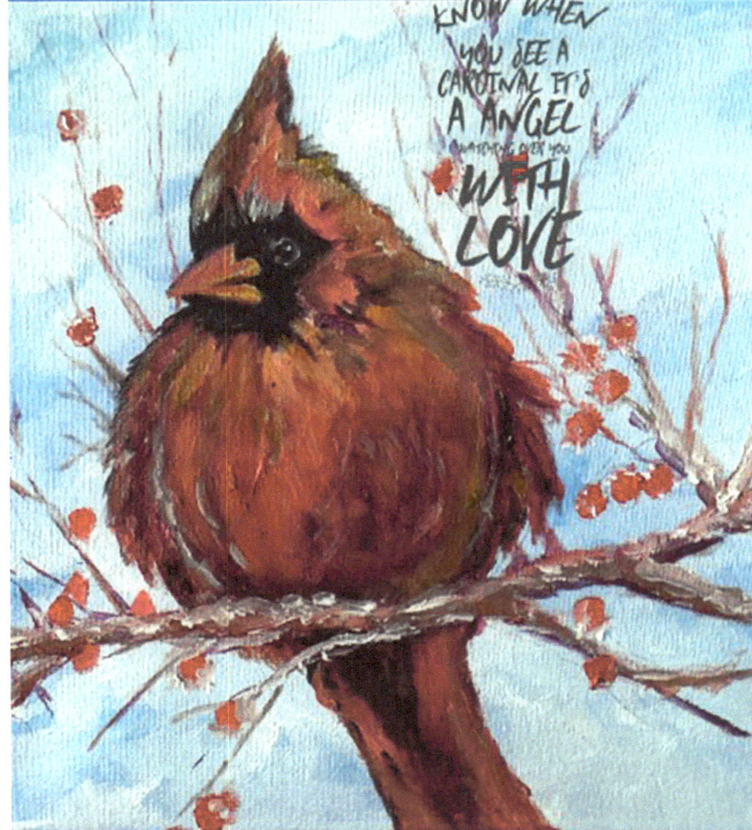

Love You, Joe

Art Therapy and DBT were the tools that helped me break the barriers of my fears and anxieties. Every lesson learned and every brush stroke made offered an alternative to talk therapy. The Art Therapy was my safe way to explore and express the memories I had. The DBT was the tool which opened the doors for me to learn to express my internal experience. These two modalities of therapy gave me my life back—not just my laughter, not just my paintings, but an opportunity to enjoy and experience life—a life that I can share with others, and a life with a loving husband and our children, friends, and family.

Neal walked in his office for my first therapy session, said, "We don't just talk in here, we work." I would have never thought, at that moment, that with his help, along with the connection of Art Therapy and Dialectical Behavior skills, that I would find the life worth living again….

Resources

American Art Therapy Association (AATA): *The American Art Therapy Association is a not-for-profit, professional and educational organization dedicated to the growth and development of the Art Therapy profession, Founded in 1969. Website: www.arttherapy.org*

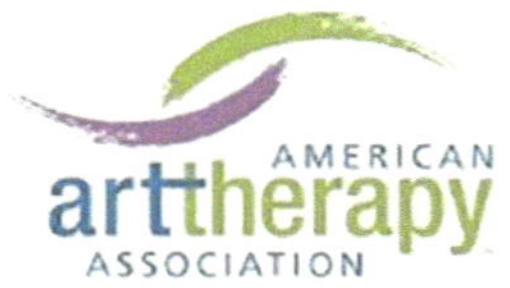

Dialectical Behavior Therapy Skills – Card Deck by Mathew McKay

Marsha M. Linehan

    DBT Skills Training, Handouts and Worksheets

    DBT Skills Training,Training Manual

Anorexia Nervosa: A Guide to Recovery, by Lindsey Hall and Monika Ostroff.

Art Heals: How Creativity Cures the Soul, by Shaun McNiff.

Art Therapy Sourcebook, by Cathy A. Malchiodi.

Become What You Are, by Alan Watts.

Building a Life Worth Living: A Memoir, by Marsha M. Linehan.

Bulimia: A Guide to Recovery, by Lindsey Hall and Leigh Cohn.

Creative Interventions with Traumatized Children, by Cathy A. Malchiodi.

DBT – Informed Art Therapy: Mindfulness, Cognitive Behavior Therapy, and the Creative Process, by Susan M. Clark.

Embody: Learning to Love Your Unique Body (and quiet that critical voice!), by Connie Sobczak.

Introduction to Art Therapy: Sources & Resource, by Judith A. Rubin.

Present Moment Wonderful Moment: Mindfulness Verses for Daily Living, by Thich Nhat Hanh.

For books on eating disorders:

https://www.gurze.com/eating-disorders/

Information about Mount Mary University, Milwaukee, Wisconsin: Art Therapy Department:

    www.mtmary.edu/majors-programs/undergraduate/art-therapy/index.html

    www.mtmary.edu/majors-programs/graduate/art-therapy/index.html

Dr. Laura Lees, Lees Psychological Services, Milwaukee, Wisconsin.

Neal Moglowsky, Center for Behavioral Medicine, Brookfield, Wisconsin.

ABOUT THE AUTHOR

Kathleen Kaufman, MA-ATR, has worked in the Art Therapy and educational fields as a therapist, teacher, administrator, education consultant, and workshop presenter for over 35 years.

Her work has focused on the Visual Arts and helping individuals with mental, physical, and behavioral disabilities. She uses art media as a tool to help individuals achieve personal awareness and give them new opportunities that can open doors to success. The art process and inner exploration can enrich the lives of many people.

Mrs. Kaufman is a member of the American Art Therapy Association as a licensed Registered Art Therapist (ATR). Additionally, she earned a bachelor's degree in art education / special education, specializing in adaptive art and assistive technology. Mrs. Kaufman holds a master's degree in administration / education along with her Principal License.

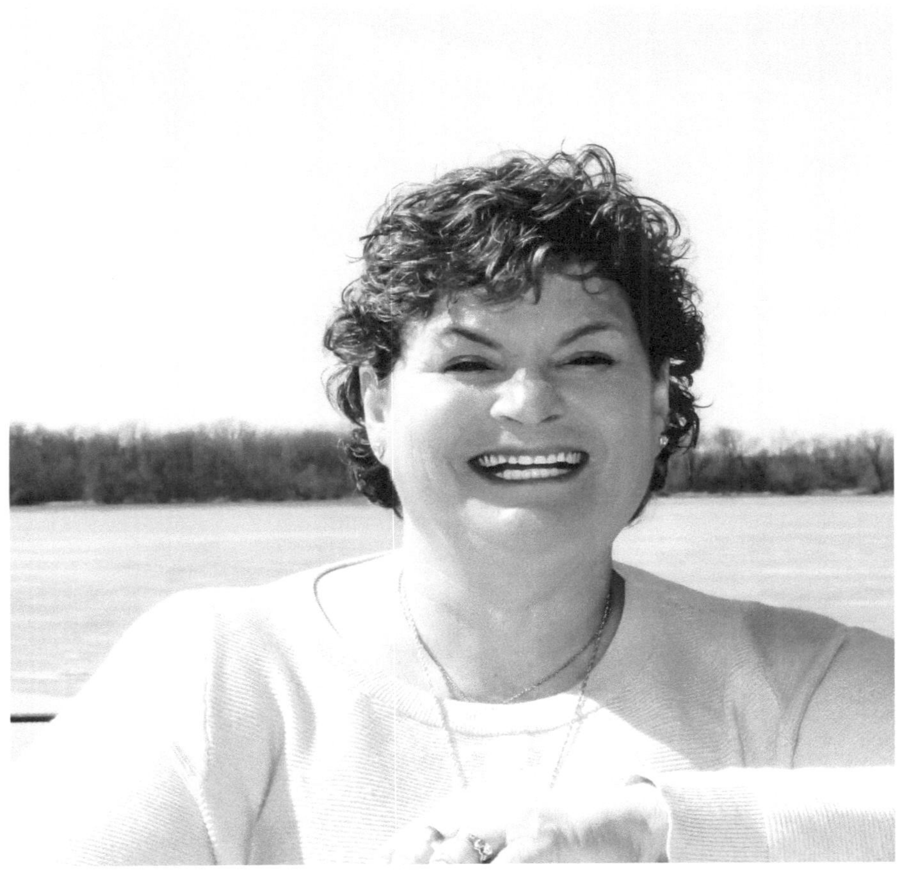

She currently owns Healing Thru Art, WI, which provides Art Therapy and Art Sessions for individuals with physical and developmental disabilities, specializing in autism and children with chronic illnesses.

Website: www.healingthruart.net